Rodgers Investment Consulting
12 St. Clair Ave., E.
P.O. Box 69042
M4T 3A1

CANADIAN CATALOGUING IN PUBLICATION DATA

Rodgers, S. Kelly (Susan Kelly), 1956-
The insider's guide to selecting the best money manager
ISBN 0-9697441-0-2

1. Portfolio management - Evaluation. 2. Investment advisers - Canada. I. Title
H64529.5.R63 1993   332.6'2   C93-094898-X

Editor: Peggy Forde
Cover Design: The Communications Group
Typesetting: The Graphicshoppe Limited
Printed in Canada

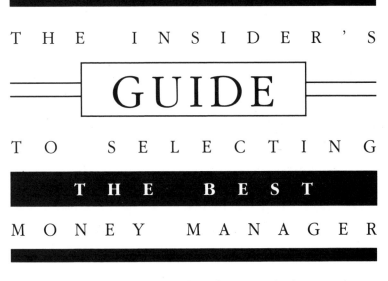

THE INSIDER'S

GUIDE

TO SELECTING

THE BEST

MONEY MANAGER

S. KELLY RODGERS, CFA

ACKNOWLEDGEMENTS

Many people have provided advice, support and encouragement throughout the writing of this book and I wish to acknowledge their contributions.

From the beginning of an idea through to the completion of the manuscript, the following friends and associates provided the encouragement to begin this project and the support to complete it; Scott Blair, Laura Buchanan, Carolyn Cross, Paul Devlin, Connie Elder, Michael Elder, Lori Ferguson, Alan Forde, Mary Hatch, Katherine Polstle Hayes, Don Howie, Mili Kus, Sylvia Lai, Kathleen Lang, Chris Lowry, Lucy Mule, Barbara Nelles, Kirk Shearer, Gord Stein, Carole Taylor and my family. To all of you, I extend my sincere appreciation and heartfelt thanks.

Many professionals in the investment industry have generously contributed ideas, suggestions and material to complete this project. Special thanks are due to the following individuals and firms: Gary Brent, T.A.L. Private Management Ltd.; Keith Douglas, Ontario Association of Investment Counsel; Mark Gaskin, Beutel, Goodman & Co. Ltd.; Ted Harris and Mary Hallward, McLean Budden Ltd.; Steven Kelman, Dynamic Fund Management; James Knowles, Portfolio Analytics Ltd.; Jean-Luc Landry and Estelle Lalone, Bolton Temblay Inc.; David Mather, Elliott & Page Ltd.; John Moore, Sceptre Investment Counsel Ltd.; Ellen Roseman, The Globe and Mail Report on Business; Sharee Ryan, Phil Evans and Linda MacDonald, Comstat Capital Sciences; Nugent Schneider and Roger Glassco, Vestcap Investment Management Inc.; Patrick Walsh, SEI Financial Services Limited; J.J. Woolverton, Guardian Capital Inc.

Special thanks are due to Peggy Forde who as editor is responsible for pulling this book together and making it readable, and to Wayne Uttley and the Graphicshoppe for taking care of all the production details.

ABOUT THE AUTHOR

Kelly Rodgers has spent over a decade in the financial services industry specializing in discretionary investment management for individuals and tax-exempt organizations. She has acted as an advisor to charities, foundations and individuals in setting investment objectives and developing investment policy statements. An informative speaker, Ms. Rodgers has addressed organizations and professional groups about investment issues and the manager selection process. In addition to managing portfolios on behalf of clients, she has extensive experience in the marketing of investment management services.

Ms. Rodgers obtained a Bachelor of Arts in Economics from the University of Western Ontario in 1978 and was awarded the Chartered Financial Analyst designation in 1989. She lives and works in Toronto and is a member of The Toronto Society of Financial Analysts and the Association for Investment Management and Research.

To clients who have indicated a
need for this information

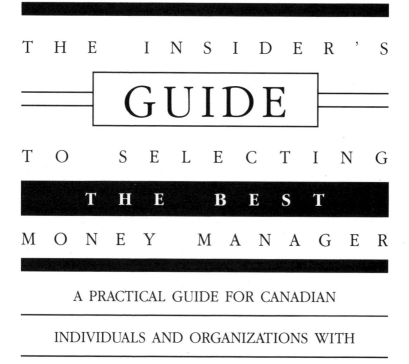

THE INSIDER'S

GUIDE

TO SELECTING

THE BEST

MONEY MANAGER

A PRACTICAL GUIDE FOR CANADIAN

INDIVIDUALS AND ORGANIZATIONS WITH

CAPITAL OF $200,000 TO $20 MILLION

S. KELLY RODGERS, CFA

TABLE OF CONTENTS

Chapter One

Introduction

Because the Canadian financial services marketplace is rapidly evolving, there is a confusing array of services and information available. With the crumbling of the four pillars of the financial services industry (bank, trust, insurance and brokerage), it is sometimes difficult to determine who is doing what. As more Canadians hold more of their wealth in the form of financial assets, the competition to manage these assets is increasing, with new players entering the fray and existing players offering new products and services.

The investment management industry has historically focused on managing the pension assets of Canadians. The growth of the mutual fund industry and the increasing proportion of Canadians' wealth held outside of pensions and real estate, has caused the investment management industry to take notice and, as a consequence, to develop new ways of serving the individual client.

Historically, the trust industry has served the individual who wanted investment management services; the brokerage industry served clients who wanted to manage their own portfolios; and mutual funds served individuals who sought professional management for assets of relatively small size. As time goes on, these lines are being blurred and new firms are entering the business of providing investment management to individuals and organizations.

Increasingly, individuals are finding themselves in the position of having to retain an investment manager to manage a portfolio of marketable securities. The client determines the investment policies and objectives under which the account will operate. The investment manager has the authority to develop and implement the investment strategy which will achieve those objectives. This service is called discretionary investment management because the manager has the discretion to act on behalf of the client in the day-to-day management of the investment portfolio.

An individual may be acting in his or her capacity as a director of a charitable, community, health, educational, trade or professional organization that has built up capital over the years. He or she may be acting on behalf of an elderly relative or friend. A fortunate few may be seeking assistance in managing their own financial assets.

Whether acting in a fiduciary capacity on behalf of an organization or an individual, or making a personal decision, it is necessary to seek out information to ensure that whatever decision is made is the most appropriate one for the particular circumstances. The seeking out of this information is called conducting "due diligence."

This book is designed as a practical guide to understanding the choices available to those individuals, organizations and their professional advisors who are seeking discretionary investment management services for financial assets ranging from $200,000 to $20 million.

The first question you are likely to ask yourself is "Why would I want a discretionary investment manager when I can use a broker and do it myself, or use mutual funds?"

For many people the answer is apparent only after a thorough analysis of their objectives and a realistic assessment of their own capabilities. Often, due to the significant size of the assets to be managed, an individual desires more personalized attention from the investment manager than is possible from mutual funds. There may be unique investment constraints that cannot be accommodated through mutual fund holdings. The overriding objective is the same — to have the financial assets under their care managed by a skilled professional on a day-to-day basis.

Many individuals have excellent relationships with their brokers but realize that these relationships are ones of **shared** responsibility. Brokers advise and make recommendations, they do not manage. One of the most common reasons an investment manager is retained is a lack of time to devote to the management of an investment portfolio due to career and family commitments or travel. Another reason is to access particular expertise and eliminate real and perceived conflicts of interest in fulfilling fiduciary responsibilities while coping with the increasing complexity and volatility of the capital markets and the almost continuous flow of economic and financial information. Finally, and perhaps most importantly, many people come to the conclusion that the ability to maintain the capital depends on different skills and experience than were required to accumulate that capital.

The key to making the most appropriate choice is to accurately define the needs and objectives of the investor and then to seek out a manager who can fulfill those needs. The choices available are many and they are as unique as the circumstances of each client.

This book will provide a practical, easy-to-use guide that will assist clients in determining their investment objectives and obtaining the information necessary to select the investment manager best able to meet their specific objectives.

Before you begin the search for the investment manager best able to meet your objectives, it is useful to have an understanding of the industry and the types of firms that provide discretionary investment management to individuals and organizations with assets of $200,000 to $20 million.

The trust companies have been, and will continue to be in this business for many years. A number of brokerage firms have specialized their business to handle accounts on a discretionary basis. The chartered banks have entered this business in the past few years in two ways: many have purchased, or set up, trust company subsidiaries, and they have also set up investment counseling subsidiaries. Some investment counseling subsidiaries of insurance companies also handle accounts for individuals. Many independent investment counselors also handle these accounts. There are, as well, a number of investment counselors which are jointly owned by a financial institution and its employees.

Within these various corporate structures, there is a wide variation in the size of firms. The industry is, in many respects, a cottage industry, and there are no uniform standards of service and expertise that clients can expect to receive. That is why each client must conduct their own "due diligence". It is not enough to simply hire the largest firm in order to make the 'safe' decision. In Appendix Two of this book you will find a listing of publications and organizations from which you can obtain the names of investment managers. In addition many accountants and lawyers will be aware of firms that handle accounts of this size and type. Although most managers are located in the major financial centres, they will usually accept clients who are located out of town and will travel to meet with the client. Whether a prospective manager is identified through an advertisment, directory, referral from a professional advisor or friend it is still necessary to conduct your own "due diligence." No one else can know your objectives and preferences as well as you do and you are the one who will live with the decision.

The structure of the Canadian capital markets is such that smaller firms can often do a much better job of meeting client objectives. There are reverse economies of scale within the Canadian equity markets. It is difficult for large investment managers to invest in more than forty to sixty of the companies comprising the TSE 300 composite index, due to liquidity constraints. Large managers become, in effect, the market, so it is very difficult for them to outperform the market. An analogy that will illustrate this is experienced in every shopping mall during the month before Christmas. If you are in a hurry to finish your shopping, it is easy to move in and around the crowd when you are by yourself. If, however, there are fifteen people who must link hands at all times, it will be impossible for them to move at a rate faster than the crowd, because they have become the crowd.

Individuals who work within the investment management industry are generally well trained and qualified to manage client assets. In order to obtain registration with a provincial securities commission, individuals who manage investment portfolios on behalf of clients must meet certain minimum educational and work experience requirements. In addition, there is a professional association which provides continuing education to the industry.

The Association of Investment Management And Research (AIMR) is an international association for professionals in the investment industry. AIMR currently represents over 22,500 investment professionals of which eleven percent are located in Canada. AIMR serves its members through a network of sixty-eight societies and chapters in North America and abroad. One of the most visible programs offered by AIMR is the Chartered Financial Analyst (CFA) designation. Successful candidates are awarded the designation after completing a series of three examinations, taken over a minimum of three years and they must have a minimum of three years of qualified work experience in the investment industry.

An important aspect of AIMR for both members and their clients is *The Code of Ethics and The Standards of Professional Conduct* (see Appendix One). Every member of the association is given the *Standards of Practice Handbook* which provides practical illustrations describing the application of the standards. Annually each member agrees in writing to be bound by the Standards in the conduct of their professional duties.

This book has been written to provide individuals with

the tool they need to select the best investment manager for their specific situation. It is also an effective tool to use in the management of the ongoing relationship. A carefully researched decision will have the highest probability of being a good decision. It is not difficult to evaluate the information needed to make the decision. The toughest part of the process has always been knowing what questions to ask. This book tells you what those questions are and why you need to know the answers.

Chapter Two

**Separately Managed,
Pooled Funds
or Wrap Accounts**

The first difficulty most readers will face is to determine which type of account is most suitable. As with all the questions this book will raise, there are no right or wrong answers. The unique needs and circumstances of each client will determine which option is most appropriate, and no final decision should be made until after the objectives have been clarified and firms have been interviewed.

SEPARATELY MANAGED OR SEGREGATED ACCOUNTS

With this service each client's portfolio is managed separately from other client accounts. This type of management provides the most flexibility to individually tailor or customize the portfolio. Separately managed

accounts can adapt to the unique needs and circumstances of each client including ethical, moral, religious,
social or environmental constraints.

Separately managed portfolios are available to clients with
assets of $1 million and over. Many smaller firms will ac-
cept accounts with assets of $500,000 and some large
financial institutions and small independent firms will
handle separately managed portfolios with assets of
$200,000. Annual fees for portfolio management services
only, excluding custodial and brokerage charges, will typically be approximately 1% to 1¼% per year of the market value of the assets under management on the first one
million dollars. Fees will normally be tapered, meaning
that as the size of the assets increase the percentage rate
of the fee decreases.

POOLED FUNDS

Pooled Funds are just what their name implies. The assets of many clients are pooled, or co-mingled, into one
account and individuals own units in the pooled fund.
The minimum investment per client is $150,000. Unlike
mutual funds, in which clients also own units, pooled
funds are sold without a prospectus.

Firms that offer pooled funds will often offer a family of
funds that could include a cash, fixed income, Canadian
equity, and U.S. or foreign equity fund. While individual
security holdings cannot be customized, the benefits from
increased diversification accrue to all unitholders.

A client service specialist will tailor the asset mix to meet the specific objectives of each client. The asset mix is the proportion of a client's portfolio invested in types of assets such as equities, fixed income, cash and real estate. A firm that offers a broad selection of pooled funds can often provide very sophisticated asset mix decisions, offering clients exposure to markets that would not be practicable on a separately managed basis.

The client service specialist will adjust the asset mix to reflect the firm's outlook for the various asset classes at different points in the economic cycle, by shifting assets among the pools.

An often overlooked benefit of pooled funds is their exemption from U.S. succession duties. Since pooled funds are registered Canadian securities, the unitholders will not be subject to succession duties that would apply to U.S. securities owned by Canadians.

The fees charged for pooled fund management are generally the same as those for separately managed accounts.

WRAP ACCOUNTS

WRAP accounts are the new entry in the Canadian marketplace. The name is derived from the fact that all aspects of the discretionary investment management process — the investment, custodial and trading functions — are wrapped together and delivered to clients for one all-inclusive fee.

This type of account was originally developed in the United States by the brokerage industry and has been extremely successful at gathering new assets under administration for the brokerage firms that sell this product. These types of accounts are now being brought to Canada by many of the major brokerage firms. The intent of these accounts is to make available the expertise of Canada's best money managers to investors with financial assets of $200,000 to $1 million.

Working with your retail broker, an appropriate investment manager is chosen and individual investment policies are developed. The investment manager then makes the day to day investment decisions, with the brokerage firm handling the implementation of those decisions and all aspects of the client service relationship. The client receives the expertise of some of Canada's top portfolio managers but it is delivered through their retail broker rather than directly.

The fees for WRAP accounts begin at approximately 2½% – 2¾% per year of the market value of the assets under management for balanced accounts. These fees are also normally tapered for larger accounts and there are sometimes additional fees for set-up or other administrative functions. These fees are shared by the retail broker, the brokerage firm and the investment manager. The investment manager's fee is normally approximately ½ of 1% of the market value of the assets, or about twenty percent of the total fee charged.

Chapter Three

Investment Objectives and Policies

It would seem as if every client has the same investment objective: significant capital appreciation, high current income and, of course, no risk. In a perfect world this would be wonderful, but the world is not perfect. In this case the old cliché is correct: if it sounds too good to be true, it probably is too good to be true. Determining investment objectives requires the balancing of competing goals, some of which are easily defined and some of which are ambiguous.

Simply put, this is the process of answering the question "What is this money for?"

The objectives which can be defined are generally the easiest to identify and assess. They often include: sufficient capital appreciation to maintain the purchasing

power of the capital; sufficient after-tax income to provide for current living expenses; growing income to provide for expenses that are expected to rise in the future;
immediate income to fund a charity's current operating
deficit or planned new program; or capital appreciation
to fund a specific project planned for some time in the
future. These objectives can be defined, and appropriate
time periods in which to reach these goals can be
decided.

Much more difficult, is the task of articulating and com-
municating objectives that are ambiguous. Many individuals understand intuitively that they are now making decisions about capital, yet their past investing history and
experience has always been with excess disposable income. With this understanding comes the recognition that
they now need a different frame of reference for this decision making but are unsure of what it should be. A frequently heard comment is "we can't afford to lose this
money because we won't be able to replace this capital".

Often used but rarely defined is the expression 'peace
of mind' when investors give a reason for retaining a discretionary investment manager. To an individual it can
mean low volatility in the market value of the assets. To
the board of directors of a non-profit organization, it may
mean the separation of the investment function from the
operating functions. To an endowment or foundation, it
may mean protecting the integrity of the investment
process from internal board politics. For a family assist-
ing an elderly relative, it could mean having an independent outside advisor balancing the conflicting needs and
priorities of different generations. Some clients will

achieve this 'peace of mind' by having a large, well known financial institution handle their affairs; others, by dealing with a firm that is small, independent and which provides highly personalized service; while still others will only consider dealing with a firm whose only source of revenue is professional fees from portfolio management, thereby eliminating conflicts of interest and biases toward one style of management.

It is important that everyone involved in the decision to retain an investment manager consider these ambiguous objectives. If a client has not decided on the objectives or does not communicate them, it will be impossible for an investment manager to develop a stategy which will achieve them. What success is achieved will be by luck rather than by design. The more clearly all objectives are honestly identified, the more likely you are to have a lasting and successful relationship with your investment manager.

A critical component in the process of answering the question "what is this money for?" begins with the development of an Investment Policy Statement. This document will form the core of a relationship with an investment manager and is crucial to evaluating the long term success of the relationship for both the client and the manager. It is important that it go beyond vague statements and articulate as clearly as possible the full circumstances of the client. It should also quantify how the manager will be evaluated. It is impossible to determine if your manager has done a good or bad job if you haven't defined what job they were supposed to do. It is also unfair to the manager to evaluate their work with the benefit of perfect hindsight if you didn't give them insight.

The following elements should always be included in any Investment Policy Statement.

Background and Overview

Who is the client and who holds the decision making authority over the account? Does any other individual or organization have a claim to the capital or income either currently or in the future? How old is the individual or organization and how did they obtain the capital? What is their past investing experience? If the client is an individual, what is their family situation and do they have dependents? Are significant changes in any of these circumstances planned for the future?

Objectives

RISK – What is the client's tolerance for short term volatility? What is their tolerance for capital loss? What is their tolerance for variations in income flow? This should be addressed from both the financial and emotional perspective.

RETURN – What is the requirement for current income? Is there any need for non-domestic currency returns to offset specific expenses? What are the requirements for capital growth? Are nominal returns, after-inflation returns or returns relative to a market benchmark of greater importance?

Constraints and Special Circumstances

LIQUIDITY – What demands are there on current income and cash flows? What are appropriate minimum cash flows? What are the intended uses of the capital?

TIME HORIZON – When, if ever, will the capital be needed? Is there more than one time horizon — for example, an older individual who is leaving their capital to a grandchild, favourite charity or church?

LEGAL AND REGULATORY – Are there any constraints imposed by law or government regulation? This could include the foreign content limits imposed on RRSP and pension assets or asset mix parameters defined in a Provincial Trustee Act.

TAXES – It must be specified whether the client is a tax-exempt organization or a taxable entity. If taxable, what is the anticipated tax rate and are the any tax-loss carry-forwards or remaining capital gain exemption? For taxable investors, it is important that your investment objectives remain investment driven rather than succumbing to the temptation to become driven by tax avoidance.

It is useful to think of the Investment Policy Statement as a job description for your manager. If you were hiring an employee, whether to run your company or to maintain your garden, you would provide them with a job description. This job description would clearly state the goals and objectives of the job. It would define what decision making authority you as the employer are retaining and what decision making authority you are delegating to your employee. This job description would also state what objective measures will be used to evaluate job performance.

You are the client and you must be comfortable with the investment decisions your manager will make on your behalf. You must understand what it is the manager has agreed to do and what it is you have retained the manager to do.

The following Investment Policy Statements are included as examples. They belong to real people and organizations and illustrate how the information can be pulled together to form a coherent and useful document. To be effective, an Investment Policy Statement must go beyond vague generalities and checking which box applies to you. Investment managers charge a fee for personalized service and this is an important part of earning that fee.

EXAMPLE ONE
STATEMENT OF INVESTMENT POLICIES AND GUIDELINES
FOR THE ENDOWMENT

INVESTMENT PHILOSOPHY

It is the policy of the Investment Advisory Committee to retain the services of a professional Investment Manager to select investments for the fund in accordance with the objectives and guidelines established herein, and considering the following:

A. The Primary investment objectives of the Fund are safety of principal and provision of secure and assured maximum income. It is also desirable that the capital be defended against inflation, to the extent possible and compatible with the above objectives, by seeking capital appreciation without undue risk.

B. The Investment Advisory Committee believes a low risk investment management style can provide attractive long-term rates of return for the fund.

C. The Investment Advisory Committee is willing to forego those incremental returns that may arise from extreme risk-taking as the long-term growth of the fund and its ability to generate a high level of income are considered to be of greater importance than an attempt to make short-term market gains that may, however, expose the fund to a significant reduction in value.

D. The Investment Manager will have full investment discretion in managing the assets of the fund subject to the general guidelines contained herein. These guidelines, which may be amended from time to time, are designed to achieve reasonable diversification, and thereby reduce risk associated with undue concentration; and to ensure that the fund is invested in good quality securities. In judging "quality", the Investment Manager should be guided by the position of an issuer within the economy or company within its industry; earnings and dividend history; financial strength; debt rating; rate of return on capital, etc.

E. It is expected that the Investment Manager will manage the fund investments so as to achieve relatively consistent rates of return and to preserve capital irrespective of major short-term market fluctuations.

F. On a longer term basis, the Investment Advisory Committee believes that equity investments will show rates of return superior to those achieved from investment in bonds, short-term notes or other fixed income investments.

INVESTMENT GUIDELINES

The following guidelines are designed to assist in asset mix and security selection decisions that meet the Investment Advisory Committee's objectives of investing the fund in a diversified list of good quality securities.

1. Eligible Investments

The fund may invest in any or all of the following asset categories:

1) *Publicly traded common or preferred equities, including securities convertible into same and warrants to purchase same*

2) *Bonds, notes, debentures and other debt securities of:*

   Federal and Provincial Governments, including their agencies and including debt securities insured or guaranteed by same

3) *Mortgages on real property. Such mortgages must be insured.*

4) *Cash and demand deposits*

5) *Money market securities including term deposits and guaranteed investment certificates of federally insured Canadian financial institutions*

2. Asset Mix

On a longer term basis, the Investment Advisory Committee believes an average of 25% of assets of the fund should be invested in equities. On a short-term or strategic basis, however, the Investment Manager may at its discretion vary the asset mix in order to enhance potential return or to partially protect the fund value against risk of decline. The Investment Manager should be guided by the following ranges (at market value) for each asset class:

	"Normal"	Minimum	Maximum
Equities *	25%	20%	30%
Bonds	65	40	80
Short Term	10	0	40

* *Foreign equities may range from 0% to 15% of total fund at market.*

3. Equities

a) *Investment in the shares of any single company should not exceed 10% of the total equity value of the portfolio at the time of purchase.*

b) *Except during liquidation or accumulation, each investment holding should be at least 1% of the equity value of the portfolio.*

c) *In order to achieve a reasonable degree of diversification, the number of individual equity holdings should range between 25 to 40.*

d) *Equity securities should be listed on the Toronto Stock Exchange or other major stock exchanges or, in the case of a new equity issue, have a commitment to seek a stock exchange listing.*

4. Bonds

a) *Investment in the bonds or debentures of a single issuer shall not exceed 10% of the total bond portfolio at the time of purchase with the exception of Government of Canada and Provincial issues, and their guarantees.*

b) *The number of individual bond holdings will not be subject to any limitations.*

c) *A minimum of 80% of the bonds at market value must be rated at least **A** or equivalent by a rating agency such as the Canadian Bond Rating Service.*

d) *No foreign pay bonds.*

5. Short-term Investments

a) *Short-term investments with a term to maturity up to one year that are eligible for investment include:*

- *Government of Canada and provincial treasury bills*

- *Commercial paper issued by Canadian corporations and financial institutions which hold a minimum rating of R2 by the Canadian Bond Rating Service, or equivalent.*

6. Foreign securities

Investment in U.S. securities is limited to 15% of the total fund market value.

7. Mortgages

Investment in mortgages may be used as an alternative to bonds when judged appropriate for investment reasons. To be eligible, such mortgages must be insured.

INVESTMENT OBJECTIVES

The Investment Advisory Committee has established investment objectives for the fund as a rate of return requirement measured against a benchmark of financial market indices that reflect the Investment Advisory Committee's views of the appropriate longer term asset mix of the fund. These rate of return requirements are for the total fund and apply over a market cycle of 4-5 years. Calculations will include realized and unrealized capital gains or losses, plus income from all sources.

The Benchmark Objective
It is the long-term objective to achieve a rate of return at least equal to the rate earned on a composite portfolio invested:
>   15% in the TSE 300 Index
>   10% in the S&P 500 Index (Canadian dollars)
>   65% in the Scotia McLeod Short Term Bond Index
>   10% in Treasury Bills

In calculating the return from this composite portfolio, asset mix will be rebalanced to the target ratio quarterly.

Component Rates of Return
In addition to the total fund rate of return requirements, the Investment Advisory Committee will judge the Investment Manager on its ability to achieve rates of return on each asset class (Canadian equities, foreign equities, bonds) that compare favourably with returns achieved by other Canadian endowment funds.

CONFLICTS OF INTEREST
A conflict of interest situation arises when an individual or group associated with the fund, and its agents, including family members, is in a position to benefit, or is perceived to be in a position to benefit, from a proposed investment transaction for the fund. In the event a conflict of interest situation arises, the individual or group involved must immediately notify the Administrator of the fund and all Members of the Investment Advisory Committee verbally or in writing of the actual or perceived conflict of interest situation, and may not participate in the decision-making process concerning the transaction in question.

Notwithstanding the above, the Investment Advisory Committee recognizes that employees of the Investment Manager may from time to time make personal portfolio transactions in marketable securities that are also held by the fund and other clients of the Investment Manager. Provided the Investment Manager maintains a system to monitor conflict of interest situations, including a policy for internal disclosure and a system to ensure no personal benefit is derived or is perceived to be derived from transactions made on behalf of the fund, these transactions are excluded from the necessity to report to the Investment Advisory Committee.

VOTING RIGHTS

The rights to vote the securities held in the fund are delegated to the Investment Manager. It is expected that voting will be undertaken solely on the basis of protecting or enhancing the financial interests of the fund.

REPORTING AND REVIEW PROCESS

Formal lines of communication between the Investment Manager and the Investment Advisory Committee include the following:

a. A written, quarterly investment review which will include a general economic and capital markets overview, a summary of the previous quarter's investment activity, a list of securities held, classified by major asset category and showing book value and market values, an outline of planned investment strategies and performance summary.

b. Quarterly meetings which will be held at a time and place to be determined by the Investment Advisory Committee, to review the investment results of prior periods, and the outlook and planned investment strategies.

In addition to the formal lines of communication, consultations between the Investment Advisory Committee and the Investment Manager will take place from time to time by informal contacts requested by either party.

INVESTMENT POLICY REVIEW

It is the intention of the Investment Advisory Committee to ensure that the investment approach continues to be appropriate to the fund's needs, and responsive to the changing economic and investment conditions. This Statement of Investment Policy and Guidelines will be reviewed formally on an annual basis, or more frequently if deemed necessary, in order to ensure that it continues to be appropriate.

EXAMPLE TWO
INVESTMENT COUNSELOR PRIVATE MANAGEMENT LTD.
Detailed Investment Policy Statement
4/12/93

The purpose of this statement of objectives is to provide a framework for which the assets of this account will be managed.

1) The clients are Canadian citizens, resident in the Province of Ontario.

2) Revenues from the account will be taxed at the maximum (1992) rates:

Interest Income	49.8%
Dividend Income	33.6%
Capital Gains	37.3%

3) **Cash Flow Characteristics**

- Occasional withdrawals are to be expected, on an as-requested basis.

- The portfolio will be responsible for generating sufficient revenue to accommodate quarterly tax instalments of $20,000.

4) **Investment Objectives**

- The primary objective of the portfolio is for long-term growth.

5) **Qualitative and Quantitative Constraints**

a) **Asset Classes Eligible for Investment**

From time to time, and subject to this Policy Statement, the Fund may invest in any or all of the following asset categories. These assets may be obligations or securities of Canadian or non-Canadian entities.

i)   Publicly traded Canadian and non-Canadian common stocks, convertible debentures or preferred securities;

ii) Bonds, debentures, notes or other debt instruments of Canadian and non-Canadian governments, government agencies, or corporations;

iii) Mortgages;

iv) Private placements, whether debt or equity, of Canadian agencies or corporations;

v)   Guaranteed Investment Contracts or equivalent financial instruments of insurance companies, trust companies, banks or other eligible issuers, or funds which invest primarily in such instruments;

vi)   Cash, or money market securities issued by governments or corporations;

vii) Pooled Funds of the investment manager.

Detailed Investment Policy Statement

b)   Constraints by Asset Class

Canadian Equities

- Maximum in single industry group: TSE weight plus 10%.
- Maximum in single company: greater of 10% or twice TSE weight.
- Maximum of 15% in companies with capitalization of less than $100 Million.
- Specified Restrictions None

US Equities

- Maximum of 15% in a single company.
- Maximum of 15% in companies with capitalization of less than $500 Million.
- Specified Restrictions None

International Equities

- As per Investment Policy Statement and Guidelines for the investment manager's International Equity Fund.

Fixed Income

Bond Quality
- Minimum BBB rating as defined by a recognized bond rating service
- 20% Maximum in BBB
- 10% Maximum in single issuer, except Government guaranteed
- 30% Maximum in single industry

Private Placements
- Minimum equivalent BBB rating as defined by a recognized bond rating service
- 20% Maximum
- 4% Maximum in single issuer

Preferred Shares
- Minimum P3 rating as defined by a recognized rating service
- 20% Maximum in P3's
- 10% Maximum in a single issuer

Mortgages
- 20% Maximum
- NHA First Mortgage, or conventional loans with a maximum 75% Loan to value ratio

Duration
- +/- 1yr of the duration for the Scotia McLeod Universe Index

Foreign Currency Bonds
- 40% Maximum in foreign currency bonds and debentures.
- Specified restrictions are as per the Investment Policy Statement and Guidelines for the investment manager's Foreign Currency Bond Fund.

Detailed Investment Policy Statement

Cash and Equivalent

- Money market securities must be rated R-1 or equivalent.
- Maximum term of any single investment not to exceed one year.

Pooled Funds

- Within the confines of the asset mix ranges stated under item "6"

Use of Derivative Products

- *Risk Management* Forwards, futures, swaps, options or similar products may be used at all times or as circumstances warrant to hedge against interest and exchange rate risks. To the extent possible, use will be made of hedging products that are traded on recognized exchanges. Where this is impracticable, transactions will be entered into only with brokers of financial institutions of sound financial standing.

- *Cost Effectiveness* Equity derivative products involving futures, swaps or similar techniques may be used to reduce transactions costs and to facilitate the management process. To the extent possible, use will be made of products that are traded on recognized exchanges. Where this is impracticable, transactions will be entered into only with brokers or financial institutions of sound financial standing.

6) **Performance Objectives**

The primary objective by which the manager's performance will be measured is to achieve a rate of return that will exceed the return achieved by the Long-Term Investment Policy benchmark, as stated below, by 1.29% over the majority of market cycles as determined by 4 to 6 years.

Asset Class	Measurement	Min	Policy Benchmark	Max
Cash and Equivalent	91 Day Cda T Bills	0%	5.0%	65%
Bonds, Mortgages & Preferreds	Scotia McLeod Universe	0%	15.0%	80%
Preferreds		0%		40%
Foreign Currency Bonds	JP Morgan Gov't Bond Index	0%	10.0%	40%
Total Fixed Income		20%	30.0%	80%
Canadian Equities	TSE 300	10%	20.0%	80%
US Equities (Pooled Fund)	S&P 500	10%	30.0%	80%
International Equities	EAFE	0%	20.0%	40%
Total Equities		20%	70.0%	80%
Total International Equity and Foreign Currency Bond Exposure		0%		40%

7) **Conflict of Interest**

All investment activities must be conducted in accordance with the CFA code of ethics.

EXAMPLE THREE
STATEMENT OF INVESTMENT OBJECTIVES AND RATES OF RETURN REQUIREMENTS

1. The Account

The client is a long term investor group that desires above-average financial performance for each asset class, net of fees. The principal objective is to increase the long term capital value of its portfolio, and to increase its purchasing power. They recognize the inherent volatility of returns in a portfolio designed to achieve above-average performance.

2. Asset Mix

The client believes that tactical asset mix decisions are a manager's responsibility within a market cycle in order to bring added value to the portfolio. However, the long term strategic asset allocation policy is to maintain a strong equity bias. Accordingly, the manager is free to move the assets at his/her discretion within the following range:

Asset Class	Minimum	Maximum
Fixed Income	25%	45%
Equity	55%	75%

The usual asset mix will be in the middle of these ranges. To operate outside of these ranges, the manager must explain the rationale for such a position and seek acceptance from the client. In addition, these ranges should be reviewed at least annually to determine their continued appropriateness.

Within each asset class, the investment manager is free to use his/her discretion with respect to Canadian/U.S. content.

3. Performance Expectations and Measurement

The expectation with respect to performance is that the portfolio will achieve above-average returns in each asset class and market on a moving 5-year basis. Recognizing that in any single year or two this expectation will not be met, performance will be assessed relative to appropriate benchmarks. For Canadian equities, the benchmark will be the TSE 300 Total Return Index plus 2% net of fees; for U.S. equities, the S&P 500 Total Return Index plus 2% net of fees; and for fixed income, to match the Scotia McLeod MidTerm Universe net of fees. In order to measure the manager's ability to select the best asset mix as well as which market to be in (i.e. Canadian or U.S.), the performance results of a benchmark portfolio will be compared to actual results. The benchmark portfolio will assume the following asset mix:

35% Scotia McLeod Universe
27% Canadian Equity
38% U.S.Equity

In addition, periodically the portfolio will be measured relative to the performance of another balanced fund manager with an investment policy statement identical to this one.

4.   Income Requirements

For the first year, approximately $400,000 Canadian may be withdrawn from the client's account by way of regular monthly withdrawals. The first withdrawal will be April 30. Early in the next calendar year, the client will inform the manager of the expected monthly withdrawal for the year.

5.   Constraints

The client does not have any specific investment restrictions with respect to individual securities. The client expects that the manager will maintain its usual standards and limitations with respect to minimum credit quality, capitalization, diversification etc.

6.   Additional Considerations

The client is flexible in its approach to meeting with the manager but will require a minimum of one meeting every six months. The client wishes to maintain access to the manager's principals by telephone on a regular basis.

EXAMPLE FOUR
STATEMENT OF INVESTMENT OBJECTIVES
AND RATES OF RETURN REQUIREMENTS

1. **Account Criteria**
   The client is a wealthy individual who acquired his wealth through personal effort by building up a business. The business has been sold and the portfolio goal is to preserve capital and provide a constant income flow. The portfolio is $5,000,000 in size.

2. **Asset Mix**
   The client must approve the general strategy. He wishes a safe constant income flow but leaves all asset mix and security selection to the manager. He wishes the capital to match or exceed inflation.

Asset mix	Minimun	Maximum
Fixed income	80%	95%
Equity	5%	20%

   The asset mix will vary within the above parameters depending on the outlook for each asset class, but it is quite possible for either end of the minimum/maximum range to be in place.

3. **Quality**
   The Fixed income component of the portfolio will emphasize Federal and Provincial bonds of AA rating. Corporate bonds must have A rating or better and must be large, liquid issues. Preferred stock issues can be used but only of P2 rating or higher. The bond holdings should be approx. $400,000 to provide diversity and liquidity.

   The equity component will feature conservative equities with an average dividend of at least equal the T.S.E. 300 average. The sectoral weighting should not exceed double the T.S.E. sectoral weighting and no more than 5% should be in any one stock, to provide diversification and safety. Equity issues should have an active trading volume to insure liquidity. Canadian and U.S. stocks will be the equities of choice. International equity involvement will be through U.S. ADR's for safety and liquidity. The U.S./Canadian currency relationship will be considered in all equity decisions.

4. **Services**
   The client will get a full portfolio report monthly or quarterly. Personal reviews will occur regularly to review the performance and plan

future strategy. The portfolio manger is available for telephone conversation or personal meetings on a "spontaneous" basis. Should the need arise, copies of all reports will be forwarded to the client's accountant.

5. Performance
The portfolio will be tracked by comparing results to the T.S.E. and Standard and Poor's indices for the equity component, and MYW Universal Bond index for the fixed income component. The goal is to consistently out perform these indices and/or to achieve a rate of return 2-3% superior to the Canadian rate of inflation.

6. Income Flow
A monthly income of $20,000 per month is required. That will be facilitated by maintaining a Treasury Bill of five percent of the portfolio and drawing down on a regular basis.

7. Custodial
All securities will be lodged with a trust company. All incoming and outgoing cheques will be handled by the trust company and they will report monthly all transactions and the overall value and income flow of the portfolio.

8. Compliance
The client's account will be renewed regularly by a compliance committee composed of all partners of the firm, to insure that the client's portfolio objectives and the firm policies are adhered to. Any changes to the client's objectives must be in written form.

9. Portfolio Responsibility
The firm will be responsible for all actions taken in the portfolio. A Senior Portfolio manager and backup Senior Manager will be specifically responsible for the implementation of all the firm's investment policies as they relate to this portfolio. Any exception to the firm's policies (asset mix, etc.) as designated by the client will be taken into consideration in the management of the account and fully noted in writing.

10. Miscellaneous
The portfolio manager will also work with the next generation of the family to familiarize them on the goals and results of the portfolio under management.

Once the process of identifying investment policies and objectives is under way you can begin the process of identifying which discretionary investment manager can best satisfy your constraints and objectives. It is unlikely that, at this point, you will have the document in its final form but you should have begun to write down the important points in your own words.

The goal now is to identify a firm and a portfolio manager that best fits your needs without being so overwhelmed by the number of choices available that a decision is never made. There are no good or bad firms, no right or wrong choices. There are however firms and individuals with different strengths and weaknesses. The following sections of this book will identify the questions you should ask and why the answers are important.

These answers will provide an understanding of the personality of a particular firm. Most importantly, these questions will provide some insight into how well a firm has built on their strengths and minimized their weaknesses.

Always remember that, as business people, investment managers want new clients. We are all quick to volunteer whatever information is favourable and positive. To find the negatives, you have to look for them. To make a good decision and choose the most appropriate manager, you need balanced information on both the strengths and weaknesses.

Chapter Four

The Firm

Whether deciding on a separately managed, pooled or WRAP account it is important to understand the characteristics of the firms being considered. It is advisable to interview a number of firms that are obviously very different in style or size. If large independently owned firms are the only ones interviewed you will have no appreciation of the highly personalized and flexible service a small firm can offer. Some financial institutions are able to offer more international services than independent firms can. Your initial screening should be wide enough to allow broad exposure without being so wide that you are overwhelmed. When interviewing investment firms the following questions should provide the information needed to decide which firms should be considered.

Type of Firm

There are three broadly defined types of firms that offer discretionary portfolio management services. They are: brokerage firms that specialize in managing portfolios on a discretionary basis, financial institutions that manage portfolios for clients in addition to their own portfolios, and investment counselors who manage portfolios for non-affiliated clients. Within these broad parameters, there are also many hybrids including investment counselling subsidiaries of financial institutions and brokerage firms. With all the mergers that have occurred in the industry, it is sometimes difficult to distinguish the players by what they call themselves, so you must look at how they conduct their business.

Firm ownership

What is the firm's ownership? Is it majority or minority owned by a bank, trust company, insurance company or brokerage firm? Is it publicly or privately held? If privately held, who are the shareholders and what percentage does each own? Is there any potential for conflicts of interest? If the firm is independent, will it, realistically, be be able to stay that way? Will the firm be sold or merged when the founders retire.?

Revenue of Firm

Is the only source of revenue professional fees for the management of investment portfolios? Is any revenue derived either directly or indirectly from commissions on order execution and, if so, does this create a conflict of interest or bias toward more active trading? Does the firm provide corporate finance advisory services and, if yes, will this bias the firm's security selection for clients?

History and Outlook

When was the firm founded and who are the senior professional staff? Do they have a clearly articulated outlook and plan for its future? Are their future plans and outlook consistent with their history and have they demonstrated the ability to carry out their plans?

Growth Record

Has a firm shown steady growth? If independently owned, has it been able to grow sufficiently to ensure its own survival by achieving a critical mass? Does it manage sufficient assets to allow for the investments in people and technology necessary to remain current with industry trends and knowledge? The other side of growth is that too much, too soon, can strangle a firm. A firm that adds new clients too quickly risks a decline in its level of service to existing clients. There is, unfortunately, no perfect formula. Each firm should have a well thought out plan that, when analyzed, fits its unique circumstances. Its past history is indicative of its ability to achieve its current plans but it is not a guarantee.

Management Team

Profiles of the management team and any staff who will be directly involved with the account should be given to potential clients. These biographies should highlight investment and business experience, education and professional training. In reviewing this information, try to assess whether a firm has a balanced and complementary management group.

Management and Staff Turnover

The history of staff turnover is probably the most important indicator of a firm's ability to manage itself. Keep in mind that the more time spent managing its own affairs the less time it has available to manage your investment portfolio.

This is the one question to which there is a good or bad answer. High turnover of senior professional staff is bad. While it is good to see some growth and evolution in the senior management ranks, wholesale turnover of people leaves you not knowing what the firm will look like in the future. Turnover must be related to the size of the firm and its own growth rate.

To assess each firm, ask how long key employees have been there. More importantly, ask how many have left over the past five years and why. If the reason given for the departures is normal evolution, you might ask if you could contact those individuals. It is unlikely they would agree, however you may gain insight from their level of discomfort.

There are two reasons a firm would not want you to contact one of their former colleagues. The first one is very legitimate from a business perspective and is simply because that person is now a direct competitor. After all, Coke wouldn't tell you to go see Pepsi. The second reason is that the perspective the former employee would give you may not match the one the firm is giving you. However, if the individual is a memeber of AIMR you can find out where they are now and contact them directly.

Staff Remuneration

There are a wide variety of compensation structures within the investment industry and it is important to understand what a portfolio manager or account manager is being paid to do. Are they remunerated based on total assets under management, total revenue generated by their accounts, investment performance relative to market or industry benchmarks, profitability of the firm or division, or some combination of these and other factors? A manager whose remuneration is weighted toward total assets under management may have an incentive to spend more time marketing and less time servicing existing clients. A compensation structure that is tied to outperforming specific market benchmarks may subtly encourage a portfolio manager to take higher risks in the anticipation of higher returns than is appropriate for your account. When a firm receives revenue from trading activity, a remuneration package based on total revenue generated may encourage more active trading in the account than would be necessary. What is ideal is a compensation structure that is directly related to achieving the investment objectives set out in the client's Investment Policy Statement.

Operating Style and Structure

To facilitate understanding a firm's operating structure and style it is useful to examine characteristics typed by size of firm. Sole practitioners will usually be investment generalists managing both fixed income and equities. Smaller or boutique firms with up to $2 billion in assets might have two to four strong investment professionals, each with their own expertise. Medium-sized firms managing $2 to 6 billion in assets frequently have teams of investment specialists and will offer multiple products such as the management of private wealth, pensions, endowments and mutual funds.

Large firms managing more than $6 billion will offer multiple products and multiple services. Often they will try to reproduce the characteristics of smaller firms within their various product areas, for example, specialty teams for pension accounts and sole practitioner for individual clients. In some firms, client service and business development are integrated with the day-to-day investment process while in others, it is separate.

As with all the other information being collected, there is no best style. Each firm must find a style that most effectively uses the talents of its professionals and serves its clients well. You must decide which style most appropriately meets your specific objectives.

The functions that must be performed within a firm managing balanced portfolios include: Asset mix strategy; Fixed Income research and management; Equity research and management, both domestic and foreign; Client administration; Client service; and Marketing.

Portfolio managers will normally perform more than one of these functions. How much of their time is spent on each area? If they describe themselves as taking a team approach, how do their colleagues allocate their time? If everyone involved in the investment decision making process is spending the majority of their time on marketing, client service and administration and analysis of U.S. equities, they haven't learned to operate effectively. Carefully question how they allocate their time and resources internally. Whenever possible, ask more than one member of the firm to see if the answers are consistent.

Client Service

Any business person who hopes to survive in today's competitive marketplace, chants the mantra of "client service". You need to know what defines "excellent customer service" to each organization. One large Canadian investment counselor has estimated that it requires approximately twenty to twenty-five hours per year to provide excellent service to each of its clients, including the preparation and travel time for quarterly meetings. Since each year contains approximately 2500 working hours, it is easy to deduce the maximum client load each account manager can handle. This particular firm provides a very intensive level of client service, including quarterly meetings with every client. You must determine what level of service is optimum for your circumstances and then look for a firm that normally provides that optimum level.

Client Profile

What is the profile of the firm's other clients? Does it manage portfolios for other clients with similar objectives? Does it have clients with the same tax status as you? What percentage of total assets and revenues does each type of account represent? Since many firms have wholly or partially owned subsidiaries to handle clients with different profiles, such as mutual funds or private wealth, where do these fit within the overall operation? If this is a new business area for the firm, why are they entering it and what is the commitment to it?

Related Services

What other advice and services are offered by the firm? It if provides advice on tax, insurance, fiduciary and legal matters, what are the qualifications of the individuals giving the advice? Have they had specialized training or direct experience in these areas? How recent is their experience and what, specifically, have they done to keep current in these highly technical and rapidly changing fields?

Firm Survival

Can the firm survive in its current form? With large financial institutions and their subsidiaries this will not be a major concern. Even when a financial institution does experience difficulty there is considerable political pressure to find a solution that protects clients. Recent examples include the sale of Royal Trust and of the assets of Central Guaranty Trust. Investment management clients experienced little disruption and were well protected during the ownership changes since client portfolios are managed on an agency basis. More disruptive for its clients was the 1992 receivership of Haldenby and Associates, a small investment counselor located in Toronto.

Investment managers manage portfolios on an agency basis. They act as agent on behalf of the client, making buy and sell decisions on individual securities. The securities are held by custodians. You, the client, have not made a deposit in the firm as you would in a bank account. The risk you bear is the market risk of the individual investments in your portfolio. A firm's merger or sale, however, can be very aggravating to clients. It can also change the fundamental character of the organization. If you choose a particular firm because it is small and independent and you represent a significant account to it, you might not be pleased to find it sold to a bank or insurance company six months later.

The factors that affect a firm's survival are primarily financial. A number of investment firms are publicly traded companies so you will be able to examine the audited financial statements. Privately owned firms will not provide you with financial statements so you will have to do a little detective work. You can assume that every firm will tell you it is financially healthy.

It is important to visit a firm in its own offices at least once, if possible. Are its offices luxurious, shabby or somewhere in between? Has the firm made reasonable investments in itself to achieve an appropriate working environment? Has it achieved a balance between style and substance? Is there a significant difference between the reception and other public areas and the areas where the business of the firm is actually carried on? Does it have far more physical space than needed or are the employees crammed in like sardines? From these types of observations try to gain a sense of whether the firm has been able to invest wisely in its own future or whether it is living a quarter-to-quarter, hand-to-mouth existence.

Does it have a succession plan and the financial resources to implement it? If an independent firm has grown significantly, there is a risk that its employees will not be able to afford to buy out the founder's shares when the founders are ready to retire. Do they have a viable plan for remaining independent or will they be forced to sell? If a firm has not been able to grow past critical mass, will it have the cash flow and income necessary to finance its succession plans? What is critical mass?

There are many factors that will affect the minimum size of assets under management a firm needs to survive. These will include rent and lease obligations, number of employees, whether it owns and manages mutual funds, and the mix and size of its other business. Mutual funds generally carry substantially higher administrative costs than separately managed accounts, while large (over $20 million) pension and institutional accounts generate much lower revenues per dollar of assets under management. As a general rule, an established firm needs a minimum of $30 to $50 million in assets under management for each officer or senior employee, including those not directly involved in the investment process. If it owns and manages mutual funds it will be the higher end of that range. The less technology and computer software the firm uses and the leaner the operation, the more appropriate the lower end of the range will be. Firms in operation less than five years and still in their start-up and rapid growth phases will likely not meet these criteria but can still be excellent choices. Enquire as to how much progress it has made toward reaching critical mass and what its specific plans are for achieving that level of assets under management.

In gathering this information you will gain an overview of the industry and an understanding of particular firms. Each client will weight the various factors differently. After reading this section you will have probably formed some biases. These biases may have been confirmed during interviews and some will probably have been changed. You should have a sense at this point of which firms you would trust with the discretionary management of your capital. The work however does not stop here. As important as the firm is, there are other critical factors on to which we will now move.

Chapter Five

Investment Philosophy and Process

Good investment managers often have difficulty describing their investment philosophy or style. They know in their minds what it is they do and how they make decisions but many lack the verbal skills to convey that information to others in a comprehensible manner. Since the goal is to hire a money manager not a talk show host, it is important to identify the most appropriate manager rather than the best marketer. To do this you will likely have to help the manager with the communication of this information.

In the November 1992 issue of *Benefits Canada* magazine listing of 120 pension fund managers, there is a fifty word or less self-description of each firm. Descriptive words that appear with some frequency include: value – forty-one times, fundamental – thirty-seven times, long term – thirty times, disciplined and growth – tied at eighteen times each, and research – twelve times. These are great statements and it is certainly reassuring to clients to know that their investment manager uses a disciplined research oriented approach to identify securities that exhibit fundamental value and offer the potential for long term growth. However, you are asking yourself, what does this mean? There aren't many investment managers who will admit to selecting securities that are overvalued with poor prospects for growth and which are likely to go down in price, yet it does happen.

There are many different investment philosophies successfully coexisting in the capital markets. The key is to find a manager who has identified a style and has demonstrated the ability to implement that style. It should also be a style that you are comfortable with and which is appropriate to your own objectives and time frame.

There are investment philosophies for each class of assets and for the overall asset mix, and these philosophies or styles are applied within the context of the client's Investment Policy Statement

Asset mix strategy can be either passive or dynamic. A passive style would set an appropriate asset mix for each client, for example, a balanced account with a mix of 10% cash, 45% equity and 45% fixed income. As movements in the market value of the securities over time alter the percentages, the mix is rebalanced at regular intervals, often quarterly. Therefore, if the equities had gone up in value, some would be sold and the proceeds would be reinvested in cash and fixed income to maintain the balance of the asset mix.

Most investment firms and portfolio managers have a dynamic asset mix style. Rather than set a rigid asset mix, a range would be established for each asset class that sets out both the minimum and maximum weightings within the portfolio for each asset class. The portfolio manager will then alter the asset mix within these ranges based on their outlook for the returns for each asset class. This is often referred to as Strategic Asset Allocation. Another style of asset mix decision making is Tactical Asset Allocation. This style differs from Strategic Asset Allocation in that it is usually driven by computer models.

All active, or dynamic, asset mix strategies are in one way or another market timing strategies. Different firms will approach the decision from different perspectives but all will have to make a decision. These asset mix decisions will normally have a greater impact on the overall portfolio returns than any other single decision, but are also the most difficult to get right consistently.

Within the equity and fixed income asset classes, there are different investment philosophies and each client must decide which style, over the long term, will best achieve their specific objectives.

VALUE investing is probably the most overused, and often misleading, description used by managers when characterizing their investment style. Classic VALUE investing is an investment philosophy first developed by Benjamin Graham and David L. Dodd in the 1930's. When an investment manager tells a client, or prospective client that they practice a value investing philosophy, what do they mean? Do they mean Graham and Dodd Value or some other style of value investing? If they do mean Graham and Dodd then it is not a simplistic rigid formula such as market price below book value. It is a method of identifying securities whose market price is less than the intrinsic value. In their textbook *SECURITY ANALYSIS* originally published in 1934, Graham and Dodd articulated their investment philosophy. Graham and Dodd VALUE investing is based on careful analysis of all the available facts to draw conclusions by the application of logic and established analytical principles. VALUE investing promotes a fundamentally conservative approach to the management of capital.

What are the available facts that require analysis to determine intrinsic value? They include the assets, earning power, dividends, capital structure and conservatively estimated future prospects of the business. These facts are distinct and separate from the current market price. Intrinsic value is a flexible valuation tool that seeks to determine whether there are substantial differences between the intrinsic value of a business and the market price of the stock. When these differences are identified, then the purchase or sale of a security can be justified.

In his 1973 book *THE INTELLIGENT INVESTOR* Ben Graham articulated the concept of 'margin of safety' as the central thesis of his philosophy of VALUE investing. It is the application of rigourous objective analysis to the historic and current financial status of a security and a conservative evaluation of the future prospects of the business, thereby combining both quantitative and qualitative analysis.

While Benjamin Graham was developing his philosophy on VALUE investing T. Rowe Price was articulating his philosophy on GROWTH investing. In a series of articles originally published in *BARRON'S* in 1939 and further developed over the next forty years, Price argues that GROWTH stock investing was the only way to protect one's capital from inflation's erosion of purchasing power. Price defined growth stocks as shares of companies which have shown long-term growth in earnings at a rate faster than inflation from one business cycle to the next.

It is important to differentiate true growth stocks from stocks that are merely enjoying a rebound in earnings due to the general recovery from the bottom of the business cycle.

In these and subsequent articles, Price articulated the "life cycle theory of investing" as the principal means of identifying growth stocks. Companies, like people, pass through three phases in their life cycle; growth, maturity and decline. When investing in the common stock of a company the greatest opportunity for gain occurs when the company is in the growth phase. Depending on how astute company management is, this growth phase can last many years as new markets are developed for existing products and new products are created. The growth in earnings will continue through several business cycles with each peak higher than the previous peak.

To be a successful GROWTH stock investor over the long-term it is not sufficient to merely own growth stocks. Careful analysis must still be conducted to determine if the current market price is justified. As with most forms of human endeavour, market prices can reach extremes. The growth rates of all companies will vary over time and it is unrealistic to expect earnings growth at rates over fifty percent to continue for indefinite periods.

At the opening of this chapter, the point was made that many different investment styles can successfully coexist in the capital markets. In a 1979 speech to the Senior Men's Club of New Canaan, Connecticut, Mr. Robert Barker, a Partner of Barker Lee & Co. of New York addressed this point. Barker Lee & Co. are practitioners of GROWTH investing and during the nineteen fifty's and nineteen sixty's achieved compounded rates of return of twenty-five per cent per annum. Mr. Barker divulged that he understood that during the same twenty year period Mr. Warren Buffet of Berkshire Hathaway, a well-known follower of Graham and Dodd VALUE investing was achieving similar returns on the investment partnership he managed, and that it is unlikely that the two men ever owned the same securities*.

Another common equity investment style practised in to-day's capital markets is SECTOR ROTATION. This style is based on the belief that different sectors of the economy and capital markets will perform well during different stages of the economic cycle. Therefore, portfolios are constructed to be overweighted in the sector expected to outperform. Greater weight is placed on the industry weight than on the individual security selection. An example would be to overweight the interest sensitive (financial services and utilities) sector and underweight the cyclicals (forest products, metals and minerals) during a recession and reverse that posture during the mid to late stages of the recovery. A manager who practices

*Related with permission from Mr. Robert Barker.

SECTOR ROTATION will be able to demonstrate these significant shifts in sector weightings through the business cycle.

One common style few, if any, managers will publicly admit to practicing is CLOSET INDEXING. It is more common than clients realize. The reason few managers will admit to using this style is simple – if a client wants an indexed fund, it is cheaper to buy an index fund. CLOSET INDEXING will be visible in the construction of the portfolios. All TSE 300 Index groups will be represented and the portfolio will be overweighted or underweighted relative to the index. These over and under weightings will not be large; for example, the maximum or minimum industry weight might be TSE 300 weight plus or minus ten to twenty percent.

One further sytle most institutional managers won't acknowledge is MOMENTUM. This style is based on the belief that when a stock is rising or falling in price, it will tend to continue rising or falling. It is an investment style based on technical analysis rather than fundamental analysis. Since most investment firms characterize their investment process as being based on fundamental research and analysis, it is not surprising that MOMENTUM plays are not discussed. It will be visible in the portfolio construction if a client pays close attention. Securities will be purchased or sold only after price trends have been well established.

Fixed Income investing also has its own styles. Traditionally most fixed income portfolios for individuals have been managed using a passive or semi-passive laddered

approach. The maximum maturity allowed in the portfolio would be determined, for example twelve years, and
bonds would be purchased with maturities ranging from
one to twelve years. As the bonds matured, the capital
would be reinvested to maintain the ladder approach
through to the maximum maturity period.

The availability of high-powered personal computers and
sophisticated software programs has brought tremendous
changes to the management of bond portfolios. Managers
can now use the computing power of these computers
and current market price data to make comparisons between bond issues on a 'real time' basis and use this information to make trading decisions. As a result the active trading of bonds within portfolios has increased dramatically and it is not unusual to see a bond portfolio
turnover one, two, three or more times in a year.

There are mathematical relationships in the bond markets, the most basic of which is that bond prices and interest rates move in opposite directions. When rates rise,
bond prices fall and when rates fall, bond prices rise,
providing opportunities for capital losses or gains. The
longer the maturity of the bond, the more dramatic these
price changes will be for a given change in interest rates.
Another factor that affects bond prices is the liquidity of
a specific issue. Investors are willing to give up yield to
obtain greater liquidity.

In addition to the mathematical relationship that exists
between interest rates and bond prices, there are relationships between the different bond market sectors. These
sectors are broadly defined by type of issuer and they
are Federal Government, Provincial Government and

Corporate. Bonds are also ranked, or rated by credit quality, which is particularly important in the provincial government and corporate bond sectors. There are price and yield relationships between the sectors and quality levels. The lower the quality of the issue, the higher the yield must be to compensate investors for the additional risk. These differences in yield levels are known as the 'spread' and are always related to the yield on other issues. For example, a manager might refer to the spread between Government of Canada bonds and Ontario Government bonds, or the spread between Canada's and a comparable U.S. Treasury bond.

Bond managers place more emphasis on a bond's duration than on its maturity when making decisions. Bond duration is a measure that accounts for timing of cash flows from the bond as well as the value of these cash flows. Duration measures allow for direct comparisons between bond issues with different coupon rates and different interest payment schedules.

Mr. Patrick Walsh, Senior Vice President, SEI Financial Services Limited has done extensive work characterizing and defining fixed income styles. He has broken the elements of these styles into four distinct strategy components which can be practiced singly or in combination.

The first component, INTEREST RATE ANTICIPATION, occurs when a manager positions a bond portfolio to take advantage of anticipated changes in interest rates. For example, when a manager feels interest rates will decline, he will lengthen the duration of the portfolio and when rates are expected to rise, duration will be shortened.

The second component is what Mr. Walsh has termed VALUE TRADING. This involves changing the structure of the portfolio to find the highest possible yield, while keeping the portfolio duration constant and the credit quality constant. An example of constant credit quality would be restricting the portfolio to Government of Canada bonds. The manager uses sophisticated software and current market prices to determine if a combination of bonds currently available in the market provides a higher portfolio yield than those bonds already in the portfolio.

The third component is SECTOR TRADING which involves trading between issues from different market sectors. Examples would be trading from Government of Canada to Provincials, or from Provincials to Corporates. In the Canadian bond markets this strategy is constrained by a lack of liquidity, particularly in the corporate bond sector. There simply aren't that many issues available in the market for a manager who must buy hundreds of millions of dollars worth of bonds for client accounts. Managers with this strategy will normally use it in conjunction with another strategy.

The fourth component Mr. Walsh identifies is HIGH YIELD. This strategy consists of purchasing corporate bonds with high yields and holding them to maturity. Again, because the corporate debt market in Canada is very small relative to the government debt markets, there is little liquidity and the added credit quality or default risk makes this a little used strategy.

Most fixed income managers will combine two or three of these component strategies to create their own fixed income investing style.

The preceding is not an all-encompassing discussion of the various investment philosophies practiced in today's capital markets. Each manager will have his or her own interpretation of these styles and many will have their own definitions. The purpose of these descriptions is to give you some familiarity with the concepts a manager will be discussing.

A firm's Investment Philosophy is its commitment to a logical and consistent style. Its Investment Process is how it implements this style. Through the following questions, a prospective client will be able to draw out the information necessary to the decision making process. It is important to always relate this information to the investment objectives already identified.

Investment Philosophy

What is the firm's investment philosophy? How do they define their philosophy or style? Can they illustrate why and how this style has met the objectives of their existing clients?

Effective Time Frame

Over what time horizons will this philosophy be most effective? How volatile, or risky, is this style over different time horizons and during different market environments?

Suitability of Philosophy to Specific Capital Market Segments

Does the firm's philosophy work most effectively in specific market segments such as Government of Canada bonds for fixed income or small capitalization for equities? What are the risks of this style in other market segments?

Ability of Philosophy to Achieve Objectives

Can the firm demonstrate that its philosophy will achieve your stated objectives? Do they have data available from existing accounts that will demonstrate both its adherence to the stated philosophy and its effectiveness? Look to actual portfolios to either prove or disprove their statements. An example would be a fixed income strategy that is interest rate anticipation with a focus on quality and liquidity. A firm with this philosophy would have few, if any, non Government of Canada bonds in client portfolios.

Strategic Alliances

Many firms have struck strategic alliances to provide greater expertise in capital markets outside Canada and North America. Some firms have been very successful with this strategy while others have been disappointed. What is a firm's current approach to U.S. and offshore markets? What has its experience been and does it anticipate any changes? How does it see its approach to these markets evolving over the long term?

Current Outlook

How does the firm interpret its philosphy in the current market environment? What is its outlook for the capital markets? How is this reflected in the portfolios now and what changes are anticipated?

Investment Process

Most investment managers will find it easier to discuss process than philosophy. This is the nuts and bolts of how they make decisions. What is the firm's investment process? Is it a top-down (economic outlook) or bottom-up (company and industry fundamentals) approach or a combination of both? Does it buy good stocks or good companies?

Portfolio Construction

How does the firm construct portfolios? How many stocks and bonds are typically held in a portfolio? Does this change from one part of the economic cycle to another? What is the maxiumum percentage weighting for any individual holding within the portfolio?

Consistency of Approach Across All Portfolios

What is the degree of commonality, or consistency, across all client portfolios? If a model portfolio approach is used, the commonality across all portfolios should be approximately eighty percent or higher. Are different individual investment objectives reflected through asset mix weightings, individual security weightings or different security selections?

Investment Research

Does the firm obtain research from brokerage firms and, if yes, from how many firms? Does it purchase any research from independent sources? Does it make use of quantitative analysis and software screens in their security selection?

Trading Style

What is the trading style of the firm? Does it actively trade client portfolios, take a long term buy and hold perspective, or trade around core holdings? What is a typical holding period for individual securities held within client portfolios?

Compliance Procedures

What internal procedures has the firm developed to maintain the discipline of its investment philosophy and process? What review process is in place to ensure client portfolios continue to be managed according to stated objectives?

Dispersion of Investment Returns

How are investment returns generated? Are portfolios managed for total return or capital appreciation? Review portfolio valuations that show both book and market values from actual accounts to assess how returns are generated. Do eighty percent of the returns come from twenty percent of the holdings, or are positive returns being generated from a majority of the holdings? Every manager will have security selections that didn't work out but it is important to understand whether returns come from a few big winners or whether they are dispersed throughout the portfolio.

Soft Dollars

Soft dollars are commission dollars generated from the normal trading activity of portfolios which are used to pay for services delivered to the investment manager by outside vendors. It is acceptable to use soft dollars for services that are directly related to the management of portfolios. For example, a firm might use soft dollars to pay for portfolio management software programs but it would be contrary to the profession's ethical standards to use soft dollars to pay for the personal computer on which those programs run.

Does the firm make use of soft dollars? What proportion of a firms total commissions are dedicated to soft dollars? The greater the proportion dedicated to soft dollar expenses, the less flexibility an investment manager has in choosing which broker will execute security transactions on behalf of clients.

When discussing investment philosophy and process, the goal is to gain sufficient understanding of a firm's investment style that you are able to complete the sentence "What this means to me is...". Since the purpose of hiring a discretionary investment manager is to meet your specific investment objectives, the only value judgement that is important is how well a firm's style enables it to meet those specific objectives consistently over time.

Chapter Six

The Account Manager

Throughout this section, the generic title Account Manager will be used to refer to the individual who has the direct day-to-day responsibility for your account.

Account Manager's Experience

What is your Account Manager's experience and where did they gain their experience? What specifically have they done? Your account manager may have extensive previous experience managing pension or mutual fund portfolios, but limited experience with non-profit organizations or taxable individuals. Each prospective client must decide what is or is not relevant to the specific situation.

Account Manager's Professional Training

What specialized professional training has the account manager undertaken? When was this training received? Have they earned a professional designation? What professional associations do they belong to?

Current Client Load

How many clients do they currently have primary responsibility for? How many clients do they have secondary responsibility for? How much of their time is devoted exclusively to client service?

Other Responsibilities

What other functions does the account manager perform within the organization? How do they allocate their time among those functions?

Investment Philosophy

Can your account manager articulate his or her investment philosophy? Is it consistent with the firm's philosophy?

Profile of Other Clients

Is the account manager responsible for other clients who have similar objectives and circumstances, or would you be better served by another account manager in the firm?

Personal Empathy

Do you get a good feeling from this individual? Does he or she communicate a sense of understanding and empathy for your situation? In the case of non-profit organizations, does this account manager understand the goals and aims of your organization? Do you believe that you will be able to build a long-term relationship with this person? Are you comfortable entrusting your financial well-being to their care?

Chapter Seven

Evaluating Investment Performance

When interviewing investment managers, some consideration is usually given to past investment performance. This is perhaps the most misunderstood and misused part of the manager search process. Everyone wants to hire the "best" manager with the "best" performance but we are often unsure of how to relate the investment performance to the investment objectives. Mark Twain is credited with saying "There are three kinds of lies – lies, damn lies, and statistics". Investment performance figures are statistics.

Every firm will report investment performance in the most positive manner possible and prospective clients should always be a little sceptical. One recent example can be seen in one fund manager's December 31, 1992 report to unitholders. The report begins with the statement that the manager was "pleased to report the fifth consecutive year of positive returns" for all the funds under the firm's management. One of those funds is a non-Canadian equity fund and the report provided the rate of return for this fund in both U.S. and Canadian dollars. The report also informed unitholders that in the future this fund's returns would be reported in Canadian dollars only, to conform with standard industry practice. This particular fund did enjoy five consecutive years of positive returns when reported in U.S. dollars, but only four consecutive years of positive returns when reported in Canadian dollars. The manager's report to unitholders was accurate but did not convey all the information a client might want to consider when making a decision.

We all want to select an investment manager based on their future investment returns but, as none of us has a crystal ball that we are willing to share, future returns remain unknown. Therefore, the only reasonably objective data we can use to evaluate the professional competence of a given manager is past investment returns.

The Association of Investment Management and Research (AIMR) has adopted Performance Presentation Standards. These standards were developed to establish and maintain sound ethical and uniform performance reporting practices. The goal in developing these standards was, and continues to be, to help managers make complete, accurate and fair presentation of investment data thereby enabling the investing public to make reasonable comparisons.

In addition to the AIMR standards, many managers will choose to have some of their accounts measured by independent measurement services. The two major services operating in Canada are Comstat Capital Sciences and SEI Financial Services Limited. Both firms also conduct manager searches for large institutional accounts and pension fund sponsors. As well, most Pension and Benefit Consultants maintain extensive data bases on the investment performance of various managers.

Performance measurement services measure the performance of a firm's portfolios relative to the portfolios of other firms. This data will tell you how well a portfolio has performed relative to a universe of other portfolios. It does not measure performance relative to specific objectives.

It is also important to understand what investment managers mean when they talk about risk. To most people risk means the potential to suffer absolute loss. To the investment industry it means volatility. Risk is measured as the standard deviation of returns from the median or mid-point, or how much the returns vary from the median during a specific period. Again this is a measurement relative to a universe of other managers and may not have any relevance to a prospective client's investment objectives.

The third, and most important, means of evaluating investment performance is to assess how well the manager has met the objectives of the client as stated in the investment policy statement. Since performance is a historical record, the question being answered is "how well would this manager have met my objectives if I had been a client during that time period?"

This book will not attempt to fully explain all of the AIMR standards, nor relative performance measurements. Instead, it will focus on how to use the performance data when conducting manager interviews.

The performance data most useful to a prospective client is the composite investment returns. The AIMR standards require that all discretionary, fee-generating accounts be included in at least one composite. Composites are required to prevent a firm from using their highest or best performing account as a representative sample of investment returns in the firm's marketing efforts. To properly evaluate the performance data, you must understand the construction of the composites.

Number of Composites

How many composites does the firm have? There are no limits as to how many composites a firm may have. The requirements are that all accounts must be included in one or more composites and that it must be disclosed if the composite consists of five or fewer accounts. Even small firms could have ten to fifteen composites. If a firm has 125 clients and 112 composites they won't be meeting the spirit of the standards and a prospective client will have difficulty gaining useful information.

Description and Construction of Composites

What are the firm's composites and how are they constructed? Accounts with similar objectives and constraints will be grouped together in a composite. Different managers will define the parameters of their composites

differently and a prospective client will need to understand the parameters to make reasonable comparisons between managers. The following matrix illustrates a simple and straight-forward method of constructing composites based on maximum equity weightings as specified
in investment policy statements.

COMPOSITE	0%	MAXIMUM EQUITY WEIGHTING 35%	65%	80%	100%
Fixed Income - Tax-exempt	x				
Fixed Income - Taxable	x				
Trustee-Tax-exempt		x			
Trustee-Taxable		x			
Standard Balanced					
Tax-exempt			x		
Taxable			x		
RSP & Pension eligible			x		
Aggressive Balanced					
Tax-exempt				x	
Taxable				x	
RSP & Pension eligible				x	
Equity					x
Equity					
RSP & Pension eligible					x
Non Canadian Equity					x

The headings in the left hand column describe the account classification. The headings across the top is the
maxium equity weighting allowed in the account. For this
hypothetical manager the standard balanced accounts
would have a maximum equity weighting of 65% of the
total portfolio, while an account classified as agressive
balanced would have a maximum equity weighting
of 80%.

The same type of matrix could be constructed using other asset mix guidelines. The prospective client needs to know, beyond descriptive words, how the composites are constructed. After all, one portfolio manager may consider an equity weighting of 65% to be conservative while another portfolio manager may consider an equity weighting of 50% or greater to be aggressive.

Number of Accounts in Each Composite

How many accounts are included in each composite? The AIMR standards require that the number of client relationships be disclosed. If there are five or fewer, it is acceptable to make a statement to that fact rather than disclose the actual number. Further disclosures include the assets under management in the composite for each period, and the average and median size of the accounts in the composite.

Composite for Each Portfolio Manager

Does the firm construct composites for each portfolio manager? If a firm has a large number of portfolio managers and allows wide latitude in managing the portfolios, there may be significant differences in the investment returns earned by portfolios with similar objectives. AIMR requires that composites be constructed for the firm, not necessarily for individual managers. Comparing composites for individual managers with those of the firm as a whole will illustrate whether there is consistency of investment returns across all portfolios with similar objectives. In some firms, there will be significant differences. When a prospective client has been attracted to a firm due to the excellent performance of a particular account, for example a mutual fund, the composites will allow the prospective client to ascertain whether that account's investment performance is consistent with other client portfolios.

Impact of Fees

Are composite returns calculated net-of-fee or gross-of-fee? Disclosure is required as to whether the returns have been calculated net or gross of fees. If the returns presented are gross returns, sufficient information regarding fees, including custodial charges, must also be presented so that pre- and post-fee results can be determined. This will enable prospective clients to make fair comparisons among different portfolio managers.

Exclusions from Composite

How many accounts are excluded from the composite and why? A firm may exclude accounts from the composites when they are non-discretionary. An account may also be excluded from a composite if the constraints imposed by the client are so restrictive that they impede the normal management of the assets. An example of this might include a portfolio where perhaps 25-40% of the assets are in one holding that the client is unwilling to see sold due to tax or emotional considerations regardless of the outlook for that holding or its impact on the overall portfolio.

We will now turn to the performance data provided by measurement services. The advantages of these services are that the data is independently calculated and presented graphically so it is relatively easy to understand (see exhibit 1). The data that is being presented is relative performance, that is, how one manager or portfolio has performed in a given time period relative to the other portfolios in the measurement universe.

"EXHIBIT 1"

QUARTILE TERMINOLOGY

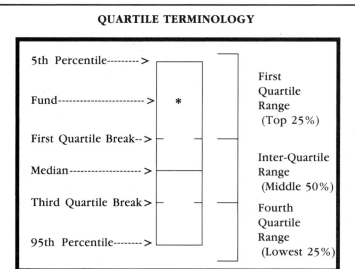

It is important to note that the difference between two quartile breaks defines a given Quartile range.

The most important range is the Inter-Quartile range between the First and Third Quartile breaks. It is denoted by the solid lines on all exhibits. If your fund falls within this range, it may be considered as ·performing average. To determine more precisely if your fund is above or below the mid-point, check your Percent Rank. If your Rank is 50 or "lower" (eg., 42), your performance is above the mid-point; if 51 or "larger" (eg., 62) your performance is below.

This mid-point is the "Median". Comstat also publishes the "Weighted Mean" which takes into account fund size. **The "Weighted Mean" and "Median" are totally different measures and cannot be compared.**

As a general statement, however, if the weighted mean for a given component and time period exceeds the median for the same data set, then the large portfolios in the data set have outperformed the smaller portfolios and vice versa.

COMSTAT

The universe will typically be comprised of hundreds, or sometimes thousands, of institutional portfolios representing hundreds of millions of dollars in managed assets. These portfolios belong to large pension funds, unions, foundations and other institutional investors. The size of the portfolios in the universe can range from a few million dollars to tens of millions of dollars. Keep in mind that these portfolios are generally tax-exempt with long time horizons, so their investment objectives may or may not have any similarity to the objectives articulated by a prospective client. These reports illustrate how a portfolio manager or firm has performed relative to other managers and firms.

The first graph you are likely to see is the total fund graph. The charts displayed in Exhibits 2 and 3 are the total fund annual and annualized total fund return for balanced portfolios. Graphics are also available for each asset class within the total fund.

Single Account or Composite of Accounts

Is this a single account or a composite of accounts? If this is a composite, how many portfolios are included? What proportion of a firm's total assets under management are represented in this measurement? What are the objectives and contraints of these portfolios, including asset mix guidelines? Can a comparison be made to the firm's AIMR composite? Is this investment performance consistent with other accounts or is this the firm's "best" account or group of accounts?

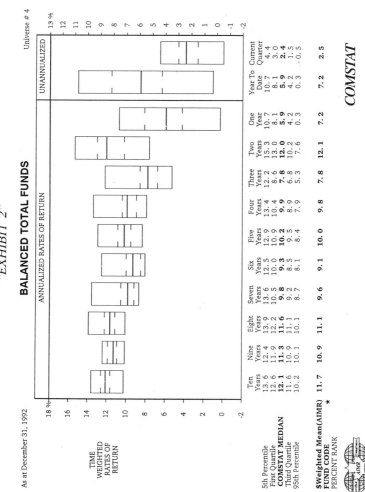

"EXHIBIT 2"

BALANCED TOTAL FUNDS

As at December 31, 1992

ANNUALIZED RATES OF RETURN

UNANNUALIZED

Universe # 4

TIME WEIGHTED RATES OF RETURN

	Ten Years	Nine Years	Eight Years	Seven Years	Six Years	Five Years	Four Years	Three Years	Two Years	One Year	Year To Date	Current Quarter
5th Percentile	13.6	12.4	13.9	13.6	12.5	12.9	13.4	12.2	15.3	10.7	10.7	4.4
First Quartile	12.6	11.9	12.2	10.5	10.0	10.9	10.4	8.6	13.0	8.1	8.1	3.0
COMSTAT MEDIAN	**12.1**	**11.3**	**11.6**	**9.8**	**9.3**	**10.2**	**9.9**	**7.8**	**12.0**	**5.9**	**5.9**	**2.4**
Third Quartile	11.6	10.9	11.1	9.2	8.5	9.5	8.9	6.8	10.2	4.2	4.2	1.5
95th Percentile	10.2	10.1	10.1	8.7	8.1	8.4	7.9	5.3	7.6	0.3	0.3	-0.5
$Weighted Mean(AIMR)	**11.7**	**10.9**	**11.1**	**9.6**	**9.1**	**10.0**	**9.8**	**7.8**	**12.1**	**7.2**	**7.2**	**2.5**
*FUND CODE												
PERCENT RANK												

COMSTAT

"*EXHIBIT 3*"

BALANCED TOTAL FUNDS

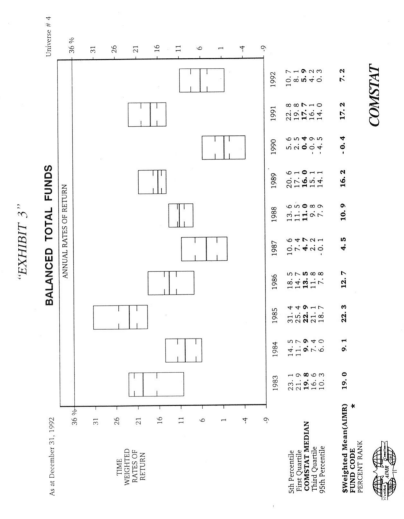

Quartile Ranking

Does quartile ranking matter? It depends. If the goal is to hire a manager who has ranked in the first quartile in each of the past three or five years then the quartile ranking is important. More importantly, one should remember that past performance is no guarantee of future performance and that it is the performance of a particular fund that is being measured, not the performance of an individual manager. Over the long term it can,be very useful to track the quartile ranking of an individual manager through the various funds they have managed. After all, if a particular individual has done an above average job for their clients over a period of ten to twenty years and they have not changed their investment style or their operating style, they will likely continue to do a good job.

The more changes a firm has undergone, the less predictive value past performance has. A manager who has excelled in running a small fund may not excel if that fund grows to a large size, or a firm that excelled when they were small may attract a lot of new money and may not be able to continue to outperform once they have become a mid-sized or large firm. There are different constraints placed on a firm managing $500 million than on a firm managing $5 billion. Some research studies have shown that a first quartile manager in one period is as likely to be a fourth quartile manager as a first quartile in the next period. What quartile rankings do tell a prospective client is where a manager ranks relative to their peers in the industry. The annual rates of return (Exhibit 3) illustrate the possible shifts in a firm's capabilities over time. It is useful to question whether changes in a firm's relative performance, either positive or negative, coincide with changes in the firm's key personnel. Relative performance is most useful over long periods of time. However short term changes that coincide with key personnel changes can be an early indication of a reversal in a firm's longer term relative performance.

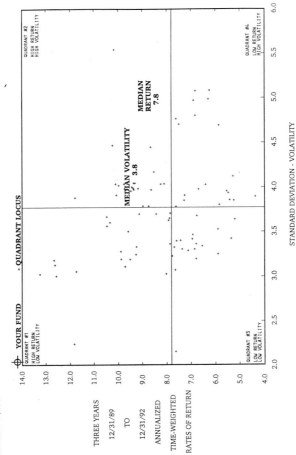

"EXHIBIT 4"

As at December 31, 1992

THREE YEAR TOTAL FUND RETURN VS. RISK

COMSTAT

Scatterplot Diagram

What does a scatterplot diagram tell prospective clients? The graph shown in Exhibit 4 is labelled Total Fund Return vs. Risk. It should more properly be titled Return vs. Volatility.

Each dot on the graph represents a portfolio. The vertical axis represents the time-weighted average annual rate of return over the three year period. The horizontal axis represents the variability of the rate of return from quarter to quarter over the three year period. Keep in mind that the volatility being measured is the volatility of a fund relative to other funds.

Generally speaking, most clients prefer less volatility to more, and more return to less, therefore one must balance these objectives. If a line were drawn at a 45 degree angle through the intersection of the return and volatility lines (Exhibit 5) one would prefer a portfolio that placed above the line. This placement would indicate that the portfolio enjoyed either proportionately greater returns than volatility or proportionately less volatility than return.

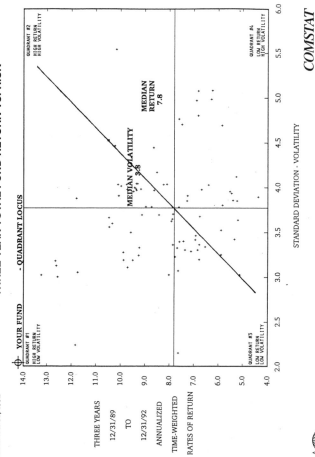

"EXHIBIT 5"

THREE YEAR TOTAL FUND RETURN VS. RISK

As at December 31, 1992

COMSTAT

Measurement Time Frame

Over what time frame should performance be measured? Investment returns should always be measured over time periods encompassing a full economic cycle, usually four to six years. When the information is available, ten year performance histories are excellent evaluation tools. Many firms that do have ten year histories have also had significant changes in key investment and management personnel during that period, so that the information may be more useful as an indication of a firm's ability to manage itself than of its investing acumen. Ultimately it is individuals, not companies, that make investment decisions, therefore performance data should be evaluated in relation to the tenure and changes in key personnel.

RELATING A FIRM'S INVESTMENT TRACK RECORD TO INDIVIDUAL OBJECTIVES

A firm could be a great firm, with stability of key personnel and superior long term investment returns yet still not be the most appropriate manager for a specific individual or organization. It may fulfill its mandate very well but that mandate may not fit with the objectives a prospective client has identified in the investment policy statement.

An example comes to mind that will illustrate this point. In the mid-eighties a non-profit organization was fortunate enough to have a substantial endowment fund which was invested in marketable securities. The asset mix was approximately twenty-five per cent fixed income and seventy-five per cent equity. This organization also ran a very substantial operating deficit for which they continually sought government funding to cover. The organization also received substantial bequests every year from the estates of individuals. Accounting rules made it relatively easy to transfer investment income into operating income but difficult to tranfer capital gains into operating income.

After reviewing the approach being taken with the investment portfolio, the board of directors developed a comprehensive investment policy. It was determined that the main objective of the portfolio should be to generate immediate income which would be used to offset the operating deficit. The board recognized that this approach would severely restrict the potential for growth of the capital funds. It was decided that this was an appropriate compromise. The organization would compensate for that lack of growth through bequests and fundraising. This necessitated a change in the management of the portfolio from an equity bias to a fixed income bias.

This change in objectives was then communicated to the investment manager. Over the next two years the manager reported excellent investment returns to the board. The portfolio's total return ranked within the top fifty percent of funds, on a two year basis and one year was in the top twenty-five percent, as measured by an independent measurement service.

At the end of the two year period, the manager was fired and a new manager was hired. Why fire a manager who was delivering superior investment returns relative to other managers? The manager was doing an extremely poor job at meeting the objectives of the client. The superior total return was generated primarily from capital gains and at the end of the period the portfolio was still invested over sixty-five percent in equities. The manager did not meet the main client objective of generating current income. This anecdote is related to illustrate the point that good investment performance relative to other managers doesn't mean much if the objectives of the client are not being met.

Importance of absolute return and relative return

The prospective client must decide whether absolute returns or relative returns are most relevant to their own evaluation process. There are many situations involving non-profit boards of directors and fiduciary accounts where relative performance is important. Determine whether the relative performance is relative to other managers or relative to a benchmark or market index. If absolute performance is more important, then look at both the nominal and real, or after inflation, returns.

Loss averse vs. risk averse

How comfortable will an individual or organization be with loss of capital and with volatility of returns which can occur within short periods of time? Most managers will claim to be both loss averse and risk averse but, as a general guideline, the higher the return promised by the manager, the higher the risk being taken to achieve that return. Ask the investment manager to demonstrate, with actual portfolio histories, how they avoided negative returns for existing clients, or reduced the volatility of portfolios under management.

Use of Benchmarks to evaluate performance

Benchmarks are often used to assess whether a manager added value to the investment process over and above what an investor would have received with a passive or indexed strategy. When evaluating an investment manager's performance relative to a benchmark, it is important to ensure the benchmark chosen is related to the stated investment objectives and constraints. Examples of relevant benchmarks include the TSE 300 Index for Canadian equities or the S&P 500 Index for U.S. equities. An example of an inappropriate benchmark would be the ScotiaMcLeod Long Bond Index if the Investment Policy Statement restricts the manager from investing in bonds with maturities of longer than ten years. It would be more appropriate to use the ScotiaMcLeod Mid Term Bond Index as the benchmark. Benchmarks must be related to the client's investment objectives and constraints rather than the manager's current investment strategy. For clients who have long term time horizons it is often appropriate to construct a benchmark using long term rates of return for each asset class based on the client's own asset mix policy.

The following tables will assist clients in determining realistic rate of return targets. Table 1 shows the average annualized rate of return for periods of from one to twenty years for each major asset class. Table 2 shows the annual rate of return in each of the past twenty years for the same asset classes. These tables demonstrate that while long term rates of return are positive, the variability of returns, both positive and negative, from one period to the next can be extreme.

Table 1
Average Annualized Rates of Return
Total Return (Cdn. $)

Period ended 12/31/92	TSE 300 (%)	S&P 500 (%)	MSCI EAFE (%)	SMI Bond Universe (%)	SMI Long Bond Universe (%)	Cdn. 90 Day T-Bill (%)	CPI (%)
1 yr.	-1.4	18.4	-3.1	9.8	11.6	7.1	2.1
2 yr.	5.1	24.0	4.2	15.8	18.2	8.4	3.0
3 yr.	-2.0	14.2	-5.8	13.0	13.4	10.1	3.6
4 yr.	3.4	17.5	-2.7	12.9	13.8	10.7	4.0
5 yr.	4.9	15.3	1.1	12.3	13.3	10.4	3.9
6 yr.	5.0	12.4	3.7	10.9	11.3	10.1	3.9
7 yr.	5.6	13.1	11.1	11.4	12.1	10.0	4.0
8 yr.	7.8	16.1	16.8	12.6	13.9	10.0	4.0
9 yr.	6.7	15.1	16.7	12.8	14.2	10.1	4.0
10 yr.	9.2	16.5	17.5	12.7	13.7	10.1	4.1
15 yr.	12.2	16.6	16.4	N.A.	11.8	11.3	6.1
20 yr.	9.4	12.7	13.3	N.A	10.7	10.3	6.9

All data supplied by Comstat Capital Sciences.

TSE 300	—	TSE 300 Composite Index
S&P 500	—	Standard & Poor's 500 Composite Index
MSCI EAFE	—	Morgan Stanley Capital International, Europe, Australia, Far East
SMI Bond-Universe	—	Scotia McLeod Bond Universe
SMI Long bond Universe	—	Scotia McLeod Long Bond Universe
CDN. 90 Day T-Bill	—	Canadian 90 Day Treasury Bill
CPI	—	Consumer Price Index

Table 2
Annual Rates of Return
Total Return (Cdn. $)

Year ended 12/31/	TSE 300 (%)	S&P 500 (%)	MSCI EAFE (%)	SMI Bond Universe (%)	SMI Long Bond Universe (%)	Cdn. 90 Day T-Bill (%)	CPI (%)
1992	-1.4	18.4	-3.1	9.8	11.6	7.1	2.1
1991	12.0	29.8	12.0	22.1	25.3	9.8	3.9
1990	-14.8	-3.0	-23.1	7.5	4.3	13.5	5.1
1989	21.4	27.8	7.5	12.8	15.2	12.3	5.2
1988	11.1	6.9	17.8	9.8	11.3	9.4	4.0
1987	5.9	-1.0	17.8	4.0	1.8	8.4	4.1
1986	9.0	17.1	67.9	14.7	17.2	9.4	4.2
1985	25.1	39.4	66.1	21.2	26.7	9.9	4.4
1984	-2.4	12.8	15.0	14.7	16.9	11.5	3.8
1983	35.5	24.0	25.0	11.5	9.6	9.7	4.5
1982	5.5	25.8	-1.0	35.36	45.8	15.1	9.2
1981	-10.2	-5.5	-4.7	4.20	-2.0	19.8	12.1
1980	30.1	35.5	20.3	6.57	2.1	13.1	11.1
1979	44.7	16.5	0.7	N.A.	-2.8	11.7	9.6
1978	29.7	15.8	39.6	N.A.	4.0	8.3	8.4
1977	10.7	.6	24.1	N.A.	10.3	8.0	9.4
1976	11.0	22.8	-0.9	N.A.	11.9	9.1	5.8
1975	18.4	42.6	34.7	N.A.	20.1	73	9.5
1974	-25.9	-27.8	-26.3	N.A.	-11.1	5.7	12.2
1973	.2	-14.4	-16.4	N.A.	-2.2	5.8	9.3

All data supplied by Comstat Capital Sciences

TSE 300	— TSE 300 Composite Index
S&P 500	— Standard & Poor's 500 Composite Index
MSCI EAFE	— Morgan Stanley Capital International, Europe, Australia, Far East
SMI Bond-Universe	— Scotia McLeod Bond Universe
SMI Long bond Universe	— Scotia McLeod Long Bond Universe
CDN. 90 Day T-Bill	— Canadian 90 Day Treasury Bill
CPI	— Consumer Price Index

Chapter Eight

Custodial and Brokerage Services and Charges

A discretionary investment manager makes the day-to-day investment decisions for client portfolios. These decisions are then executed by an investment dealer or broker. The securities are held by a custodian and are registered in street name so that they are easily transferable. If the investment manager hired is an investment counselor, these three functions are performed by three separate companies and each is paid separately. If an institution, such as a trust company, is hired as the investment manager, the institution will usually provide both the investment management and custodial services. Investment counselors and institutions execute security transactions on behalf of clients through a wide variety of brokerage firms in North America and abroad. When a brokerage firm is retained as investment manager, the firm will normally provide the custodial services and execution of substantially all of the security transactions.

Regardless of how the services and fees are packaged there are charges for each part of the process. The most straightforward are the investment counselors and the brokerage sponsored WRAP accounts.

Brokerage sponsored WRAP accounts charge one all-inclusive fee for the management, trade execution and custodial functions. Depending on the brokerage firm, the fee for balanced account management will be approximately 2½% to 3% of the market value of the assets under management.

Investment counselors will separate the charges for each part of the investment process. Fees for the investment management generally begin at 1% to 1¼% of the market value of the assets under management. The charges for custodial services are charged directly by the custodian and generally range from ¼ to ½ of 1% of the assets. There are normally additional administrative charges each time a transaction occurs. For the purpose of these charges, maturity of treasury bills, buys and sells, and receipt of interest and dividends are all considered transactions. These charges are generally quite low but can add up if there is a high level of activity or if the account is relatively small.

The third area of charges is the brokerage commissions for buying and selling securities. The commissions are added to the price of the stock on purchases and deducted from the proceeds on sales. Most investment counselors negotiate institutional commission rates which range from ¼ to ½ of 1% of the value of the trade. Obviously the more actively traded the portfolio the greater the cumulative total of these administrative and brokerage charges.

Some investment managers do not charge separate custodial fees. These are the brokerage firms who manage accounts on a discretionary basis or those which have some affiliation with a brokerage firm. Rather than charge for custodial services separately, the fee is included as part of the brokerage service. Security transactions will be charged retail commission rates for execution, generally 2% of the value of the trade. Some firms will execute trades at a discount from retail rates. However, even a fifty percent discount from retail rates is still two to four times greater than institutional rates.

In the investment business, as in all others, there is no free lunch. All charges will affect the returns earned by the portfolio. It is important to understand what all the charges are in order to determine if fair value is being received. You must decide if the fees and costs are reasonable compared to the alternatives and commensurate with the service and investment returns received.

Chapter Nine

Managing the Relationship

Now that you have used this guide to identify and hire the most appropriate manager, you can begin the process of managing the relationship. We live in a dynamic and ever-changing world and must be prepared to deal with changes in objectives and within the investment firm.

One always hopes the relationship with one's investment manager will be long term. However, this expectation must be tempered with the realization that circumstances and firms change.

The key to a successful relationship is regular and effective communication. It is the client's responsibility to regularly update the manager regarding changes in objectives and circumstances. It is, or should be, the manager's responsibility to regularly report on how well the stated objectives are being met. In the early years of the relationship, meetings should be held quarterly. This may seem tedious at times but it is during these face-to-face meetings that the client and the manager have the opportunity to get to know each other. These meetings should be more than a straight report on investment returns. Time should be spent relating the investment returns and activity to the client's stated objectives. The investment manager should be using these meetings to learn more about the organization or individual behind the account.

The client should use these meetings to elicit information about the firm, its growth, and its evolving character. A firm is a collection of individuals and, as such, it is dynamic. Firms grow and change just as individuals do. All large firms started out small. As a firm moves through its own life cycle from small and rapidly growing, to mid-size and growing steadily, to large and mature, one must assess whether the firm is still able to meet the objectives outlined.

As the objectives of the client evolve, judgements will have to be made about the continued appropriateness of the investment manager. Decisions about money management can take on a very emotional character. By using quarterly meetings to gain information about the manager and relating this information to the investment objectives, you can reduce or eliminate the emotional part of the decision making process.

The Investment Policy Statement should be formally reviewed annually and either be confirmed or revised.

Investment returns should be evaluated quarterly on a rolling three to five year time frame. Investment returns must always be evaluated within the context of the objectives, constraints and time horizon identified in the policy statement.

Review, annually, the updated AIMR performance data that was evaluated in the initial decision to hire the investment manager. Are the returns in the portfolio consistent with the composite returns for other accounts with similar objectives? If the returns are not consistent, find out why.

WHEN TO CHANGE THE INVESTMENT MANAGER

Review the reasons for hiring a particular investment manager bi-annually to determine if those reasons are still valid. Investment firms are not static organizations and the relationship between an investment manager and a client is not a static one. There is a delicate trade-off between maintaining the stability of the relationship and being prepared to change investment managers when circumstances dictate.

Although no one likes to consider the possibility, there will likely come a time when it is appropriate to change investment managers. This decision should be made within the context of the client's objectives, constraints and time horizon. **One certain way to ensure long term sub-par investment performance is to change investment managers frequently, chasing after the short term star performers.** Chasing after short term performance usually ensures that one is firing the manager one should be hiring and vice-versa.

Even when the focus of the evaluation is on the long term objectives, there may still come a time when a change in manager is necessary and appropriate. It can be a wrenching experience to fire your investment manager, particularly if the firm is small and your account represents a significant part of the firm's business. The difficulty of the situation will be contained if you keep in mind that the new investment manager is better able to meet your objectives. This is a business relationship and if one supplier is unable to deliver a quality product that provides value then you change suppliers.

It can be difficult to know with certainty that a change in investment manager is appropriate. Often there is a vague feeling of unease, and signals that become obvious in hindsight. The time to change managers is when these signals start to appear, long before the evidence becomes overwhelming and your portfolio has suffered substantial negative consequences.

The following is a list of the most common early warning signals that indicate a firm is having trouble. Clients should monitor the situation closely and be prepared to take action if appropriate. The impact that difficulties can have on a firm include lower profitability, sale of the controlling interest to an institution, or closure of the firm. The impact these difficulties can have on a client include substandard investment returns, failure to meet investment objectives and additional worry and concern over one's financial well-being. The client will have to weigh the potential consequences and make decisions appropriate to individual circumstances. The following warning signals, if noticed, will assist in timely decision-making.

Inability to manage the portfolio to stated objectives

This may seem obvious. However, it is often difficult to isolate. As a firm grows, it undergoes changes in its own character and style and in what it can realistically accomplish for its clients. The most obvious example is the firm that begins small and aggressive with a mandate to deliver superior investment returns. In doing well and fulfilling this mandate they attract many new clients and quickly grow to be a large firm. The catch twenty-two is that the larger the firm is, the less it is able to add value in the way it could as a small firm. Due to sheer size, it is unlikely that the firm will be able to meet the objectives of a client seeking flexible, aggressive, performance-oriented investment management.

Turnover in key personnel

This signal will be the one most visible to existing clients. Even if the turnover and changes do not affect you directly, it is still the strongest indicator that a firm is having difficulty. You should ask the account manager to provide an update on any changes in key personnel within the organization as a whole, at least once a year.

Changes in written reporting packages

Many firms will strive to enhance the written reports that are provided to clients, so periodic changes should be expected in the reporting package. These changes should be clearly explained and you should fully understand why the changes have been made. Sufficient information should be provided to allow for direct comparisons with prior periods.

Two examples of changes in reporting that can be cause for concern are changes in currency reporting of non-domestic holdings and changes in reporting benchmarks. When a manager who has been reporting non-domestic holdings in U.S. dollars switches to valuing those holdings in Canadian dollars, the reason for the change should be clearly explained. In addition, values in both currencies should be provided for at least four consecutive quarters (one year) to allow you to make direct comparisons with prior periods. This will ensure that poor investment results are not being masked or hidden by currency effects.

Managers will often use benchmarks of some type in reports to clients and in quarterly letters to prospective clients and their professional advisors. These benchmarks may be well known indexes or could be relative rankings by pension fund measurement services or the monthly mutual fund rankings found in the daily business press. Whatever benchmark is used, it should be relevant to the objectives of the client and must be consistent every quarter, both in terms of the construction of the benchmark and the time frames reported. When either the construction of the benchmark changes or the time periods reported change, it may signal that the investment manager is attempting to hide poor investment returns. Normal reporting time periods are current quarter, one, two, three, four and five years.

Written quarterly portfolio reports and valuations should be easily reconcilable with the reports provided by the custodian. Difficulty in reconciling the two sets of reports are a strong signal that problems exist within the firm.

Change in the level or style of service

Changes in the level or style of service is the best leading indicator of the future direction of the firm. It is also one of the more difficult indicators to pin down.

Service can decline because a firm has added too many accounts too quickly and increases in staff have not kept pace. This is always a potential risk when the account manager's remuneration is based on the total size of the assets under their direct responsibility.

Another common reason that service will decline is that a firm is experiencing internal difficulties. When this happens, the time and efforts of senior employees are directed toward these problems rather than toward management of client portfolios, which eventually results in substandard investment returns. The warning signals are delays in returning telephone calls, a decrease in the frequency of personal meetings to review the portfolio, and a change in the style of these meetings. The more vague the discussion, or the more it seems that one is hearing a "trust me, we're still doing a good job" type of report, the closer you need to monitor the situation. The other extreme is that a manager may try to overwhelm a client with technical data and jargon that makes the whole reporting process incomprehensible.

When you have difficulty getting direct answers to direct questions, the time has come to search for a new investment manager.

Changes in investment style

An investment manager may begin to change a success-ful investment style for three common reasons. The first is that short term results have fallen behind the target rate of return or benchmark. When this happens there is a temptation to become more aggressive or to assume a higher level of risk than is appropriate, in an effort to recoup any shortfall in returns. The trading activity in the account may increase or the security selections may have the characteristics of momentum plays.

The second reason a firm may change the investment style is due to a change in the stage of the firm's own life cycle. A firm that has grown dramatically may now have so many assets under management that investments can only be made in the largest and most liquid securi-ties. This is particularly true in the Canadian capital markets.

The third reason for a change in style is related to changes in key personnel. When a senior portfolio manager joins a firm, they will often bring their own investment style which may differ from the firm's existing style. As new securities are added to the portfolio, you will often see differences in the characteristics of the holdings. Exam-ples include security selection based on sector rotation or momentum, when the firm has historically focused on growth, or a switch in style from value to growth. This can also be seen in fixed income portfolios and would be evidenced by moves from government bonds to the corporate bond sector or in moves to the extremes of the bond market maturity schedule.

It is important to identify these style changes early in order to assess the probable long term impact, the firm's ability to be successful with this new style and, most importantly, the appropriateness of these changes to your investment objectives and constraints.

Changes in trading activity

Increases in trading activity can be a signal that investment returns have fallen behind the target return and the investment manager is trying to recoup lost ground.

When a firm receives revenue from trading commissions, increased trading activity can be a signal that asset and revenue growth has not kept pace with budget projections. Increases in revenue from commissions on trading is one method of increasing revenue to offset any shortfall in fee revenue. It is highly unlikely that this increase in activity would reach extreme levels. However, it could be more active or more aggressive than appropriate on a strictly fundamental basis.

If the investment manager is small and uses soft dollars extensively, increased trading may be a sign that activity is required to meet soft dollar obligations. At least bi-annually, ask what proportion of the firm's trading commissions are directed to soft dollars and what is the actual dollar amount. If the dollar amount is increasing while the proportion of the total is static, it will indicate that more commissions are being paid. This may be due to growth in assets under management or increasing commission rates or higher trading activity. Increases in total soft dollar expenses may be an early signal of revenue shortfalls and the firm's efforts to meet normal operating expenses.

Increase in frequency of fee billings

Mutual funds and pooled funds normally bill fees monthly, in arrears. Separately managed accounts are normally billed quarterly, in arrears. If the frequency of the billing is increased, for example from quarterly to monthly, this is a stong signal that the firm is experiencing financial difficulty. Even if the firm solves the current difficulties you can expect a period of time when the focus of the firm is on internal matters rather than on client portfolios.

Changing investment managers is not a decision that should be taken lightly. There are real costs involved in the decision. These costs include the custodial and brokerage charges incurred when the new investment manager restructures the portfolio, as well as the time and energy involved in choosing the new manager. There are, however, also real costs involved in remaining with an investment manager who is unable to achieve your objectives.

Individually, the signals outlined should be viewed as warnings. When these warning signals begin to appear, you must seriously consider whether it is appropriate to change managers. The more warning signals there are, the greater the likelihood that the firm will be unable to achieve your specific investment objectives. When there is substantial evidence that a particular investment manager will be unable to achieve a client's investment objectives then the most logical and rational course of action is to change the investment manager.

Chapter Ten

Case Studies

In this chapter, five hypothetical case studies will show how you can ensure that the search for an investment manager remains a manageable task. In developing these hypothetical scenarios, elements of real experiences and situations have been blended together to create broadly realistic situations.

CASE STUDY ONE
Jim and Heather McDonald are in their early forties and have three children. Jim is a professional engineer and Heather is a marketing manager. Their combined annual incomes total $140,000 and they have built savings and investments, both within and outside of their RRSP's, totalling $200,000.

Two years ago, Heather inherited $400,000 from her family, half of which they used to pay off their mortgage. Recently, Jim's widowed mother was diagnosed with Alzheimer disease. Since Jim's two siblings live some distance from their mother, the responsibility for managing her affairs has fallen on Jim's shoulders. A properly executed Power of Attorney has appointed Jim to act on his mother's behalf. Mrs. McDonald Sr. has recently moved to a retirement facility that will be able to provide increasing levels of care. With her pension income, the proceeds from the sale of her home, GIC investments, Canada Saving Bonds and some long held common stocks, Mrs. McDonald's financial assets total approximately $600,000 and her income requirements are modest.

Jim and Heather have always taken advantage of the benefits of mutual funds in their own investment plans. They are pleased with the results they have achieved through their participation in fully diversified, professionally managed portfolios. As a busy professional with his own family, Jim has little time to devote to managing his mother's affairs. Jim is also somewhat nervous about his accountability to his siblings for the stewardship of their mother's financial affairs.

Due to the now substantial combined size of his mother's and his own family's financial assets, Jim has decided to retain a professional money manager to manage both portfolios on a discretionary basis. Having made this decision, Jim and Heather began the process of identifying investment objectives and very quickly realized that very different objectives, constraints and time horizons applied to each pool of capital. What emerged from this process were the following preliminary investment policy statements for each pool of capital.

PRELIMINARY INVESTMENT POLICY STATEMENT

Mrs. McDonald Sr.

OBJECTIVES
- Conservative and prudent stewardship of the capital;
- Protection of the capital from the effects of inflation;
- Modest current income with the ability to increase income in the future;
- Peace of mind for both Mrs. McDonald and her children, who will eventually inherit her estate.

CONSTRAINTS
- Mrs. McDonald has recently begun to worry about her financial security and is generally unfamiliar with the investment management industry;
- Jim's siblings will be monitoring the stewardship of the assets.

TIME HORIZON
- Management of these assets will likely be required for ten to twenty years, however the income requirements could begin to change dramatically in as little as five years.

SIZE
- The assets to be managed total approximately $600,000.

PRELIMINARY INVESTMENT POLICY STATEMENT

Jim and Heather McDonald

OBJECTIVES

- Long-term, after-inflation, after-tax capital appreciation without undue levels of risk;
- Participation in capital markets outside of Canada to increase investment returns and reduce risk through diversification;
- There are no income requirements and all income and capital gains will be reinvested;
- Some volatility of returns is acceptable as they have no mortgage or other debt.

CONSTRAINTS

- The only constraint is the avoidance of undue risk;
- While prepared to be moderately aggressive investors, they are not prepared to speculate.

TIME HORIZON

- The initial time horizon for these objectives is approximately twenty years;
- The objectives will likely become more conservative as they approach retirement.

SIZE

- The assets to be managed are approximately $150,000 in RSP's and $325,000 outside the RSP's

In reviewing the two sets of investment objectives it becomes apparent that there are significant differences in what each hopes to achieve. Jim has begun to wonder if it is possible for one manager to handle both accounts.

To assist with this decision Jim developed the following for his mother's account and his own account to identify the characteristics of a firm or manager that are appropriate for each situation.

Mrs. McDonald Sr.

CHARACTERISTICS/CRITERIA

Well known
- peace of mind and mental comfort gained from familiarity for both Jim's mother and siblings.

Longevity
- it could be upsetting for Mrs. McDonald and therefore difficult to change firms in the future.

Administrative capabilities
- bill paying and tax preparation services may be required.

Conservative
- the objective is conservative stewardship;
- prefer low risk, low volatility even if that results in lower returns.

Other expertise
- may require advice and guidance to fully understand legal responsibilities when acting under Power of Attorney.

Avoidance of conflicts
- revenue from professional fees only to avoid any real or perceived conflicts or bias in the handling of the account.

Jim and Heather McDonald

CHARACTERISTICS/CRITERIA

Flexible/Dynamic/Aggressive
- the focus is on long term superior performance.

Smaller rather than larger
- understand that there are inherent reverse economies of scale in the Canadian equity markets.

Demonstrated results
- more concerned with results than with how well known a firm is;
- want to avoid closet indexing.

Service
- as professionals they expect high level of service.

International exposure
- believe in broad geographic diversification

Jim has concluded that the investment firm likely to do a good job for his mother is unlikely to satisfy his own objectives. In addition, the type of corporate culture and environment that will provide reassurance to his mother and siblings is unlikely to be focused on his own objectives and needs. Although some firms will claim that they can successfully be all things to all people, Jim believes that it could well be a recipe for disaster, although some of the larger firms might be coping reasonably well. For his own account, however, he would prefer to consider small and mid-size firms.

After making some telephone inquiries and discussing it with his siblings, Jim feels his mother may be best served by one of the Trust Companies. Both the bank owned and independent trust companies seem to meet all the criteria identified, and he has been impressed with the information he has received to date. Most will handle separately managed accounts with assets of under $1 million and they will certainly handle the account conservatively. Recognizing that even within the trust industry each firm has a distinct style, Jim can now set up meetings to interview three or four firms. In these interviews Jim will be seeking information about the investment philosophy and process, the ability of each organization to satisfy the objectives and the continuity of the investment process. In addition to the trust companies, Jim will make inquiries with insurance companies as to whether any offer this type of service.

For his own family's investment portfolio, the criteria identified are quite different. The choice of firms is much wider and the type of account is more flexible. Jim doesn't care whether the account is separately managed or part of a pool. He will be more likely to find the international capabilities in a large or mid-size firm, yet he will be a more significant client to a small firm. A small firm will also be more flexible in their approach to the Canadian capital markets. After further consideration, Jim decides to narrow his search to small and mid-size firms with pooled fund capabilities and some exposure to international markets. He would prefer a firm that has a slight tilt toward youth rather than retirement among key personnel. He believes professionals of his own age will bring the experience necessary while still being achievement oriented.

The next step for Jim is to request written information from firms that manage less than five billion dollars in total assets, handle assets for private individuals and have international capabilities. Once he has reviewed this information he can schedule meetings to interview individual firms.

CASE STUDY TWO

A community based non-profit organization located in a mid-size regional city recently received a bequest of $500,000. The board of directors formed an Investment Committee to investigate and make recommendations on suitable approaches to the management of this capital. Currently, the finance committee of the organization is investing this capital in treasury bills and term deposits until appropriate long term decisions are made.

At the first meeting of the Investment Committee, a number of important issues were identified and some key decisions made. The committee felt that, although some of their members are knowledgeable and reasonably experienced in handling their personal investments, they would be uncomfortable making the day-to-day decisions on behalf of the organization. There is also a concern that the board may be prone to the 'Monday morning quarterback' syndrome. Therefore, the Investment Committee decided to seek qualified outside management.

The Investment Committee decided on a two step approach. The first step was to develop a preliminary Investment Policy Statement. The second step will be to identify a list of potential managers who would be capable of meeting the objectives and be acceptable to the full board.

In developing the Investment Policy Statement it was decided that this bequest would be treated as long term capital. The organization expects to embark on a fund raising campaign to supplement this bequest and to build a capital fund over the next five years. Once the capital has been built up, the organization would expect to use all income earned annually. The asset mix will be consistent with the Ontario Trustee Act, as recommended by the Public Trustee. In addition, the board feels it is appropriate, due to nature of the organization, to impose fairly strict ethical constraints on the security selection within the portfolio.

PRELIMINARY INVESTMENT POLICY STATEMENT

OBJECTIVES
- Conservative management of capital assets;
- Asset mix consistent with Ontario Trustee Act (maximum equity weighting 35%);
- Independence of capital assets from day-to-day operations;
- Insulate management of investment portfolio from changes in composition of board of directors;
- Fulfill fiduciary responsibilities.

CONSTRAINTS
- Each individual security within the portfolio must meet ethical standards of the organization which will prohibit investments in companies that profit from alcohol, tobacco, gambling and munitions.

TIME HORIZONS
- The first time horizon is five years during which all gains and income will be reinvested;

- After five years all income will be distributed annually;
- It is the intent of the board that the capital fund will continue in perpetuity.

SIZE
- The assets to be managed total $500,000

The task of developing the list of prospective managers was more difficult. Although most board members were unfamiliar with discretionary investment management, that did not prevent them from holding strong opinions on which type of firm should be retained and each had their own favourite recommendation.

CHARACTERISTICS/CRITERIA

Well known
- Peace of mind from choosing what could be thought of as a 'brand name'.

Established
- feel most comfortable with a firm that has a long track record.

Separately managed account
- most important consideration due to ethical constraints.

Conservative
- are nervous about industry 'stars' and more comfortable with more moderate approach.

Service
- must report in person at least semi-annually on the management of the portfolio;
- would prefer to deal with someone in the community.

No conflicts
- cannot accept any conflicts, either real or perceived, with regard to order execution or security selection.

Employee ownership
- three of nine board members believe only firms with significant employee ownership should be considered.

At first glance, it is unlikely that any investment manager would be able to meet all the criteria outlined. Established, well-known firms tend to be fairly large and will not usually handle separately managed accounts for assets of less than $1 million. The financial institutions which will handle accounts of this size will generally not meet the criteria of significant employee ownership.

The investment committee had some concerns that the personal biases of individual members were hampering their task. They wisely recognized, however, that if these biases were not resolved, no investment manager could hope to receive a clear mandate and fair evaluation.

The investment committee felt, that with some compromise, there were two options that could accommodate most of the criteria outlined. The first option was to consider smaller, less well known managers who would be prepared to provide client references. The committee felt that references could be an adequate substitute for a 'brand name'.

The second option would be to use a broker sponsored WRAP account. Although the costs would be significantly higher, the committee would be hiring a well-known manager to handle the account on a separately managed basis. In addition, the retail broker in their community would be available to provide additional day-to-day service.

The investment committee decided to recommend to the board that two WRAP managers and two small managers be interviewed. After these interviews, the board could decide whether the value of the 'brand name' would be worth the extra cost of the WRAP account.

CASE STUDY THREE

This privately endowed Foundation has an investment portfolio in excess of $5 million. Until now, the portfolio has been directed by the individual who endowed the foundation and acts as its Chairman – with the assistance of his stock broker and extensive use of mutual funds. The Chairman has concluded that it is time to manage the foundation on a more business-like basis, and to put in place the structures that will survive his personal involvement. He hopes that his children and grandchildren will continue his work with the foundation, but he wants to ensure that the investment portfolio remains independent. He has decided, therefore, to retain the services of an investment manager.

The Chairman built his own substantial assets through the growth of several small and medium sized businesses, as well as real estate investments. He knows that building wealth requires a long term perspective. He wants the foundation to continue to build its capital, rather than just keep pace with inflation, in order to fund worthwhile philanthropic projects in the future. His business fortune was built on disciplined long term investing in thoroughly analyzed opportunities and he believes that this is the approach to the capital markets that the foundation should take. He also cares less about how big or well known the investment manager is than about how good it is.

PRELIMINARY INVESTMENT POLICY STATEMENT

OBJECTIVES

- Long-term growth through disciplined research and investing;
- Reasonable liquidity of investments to meet legal capital distribution requirements;
- Total return target over a full market cycle of 5% distribution requirement plus inflation plus 2% growth.

CONSTRAINTS

- No significant moral or ethical constraints;
- Distribution of 5% of capital required annually to maintain tax-exempt status.

TIME HORIZON

- The foundation has been established to run in perpetuity.

SIZE

- The assets to be managed total in excess of $5 million.

Although the chairman found it relatively easy to establish the preliminary investment objectives, it will be more difficult to develop a reasonably sized list of managers to interview for a number of reasons. One is, that since this represents a very substantial account every manager will want to handle it. Another is that the chairman's indifference to a firm's size or media profile will mean the inclusion of many small, tightly focused firms as potential managers.

CHARACTERISTICS/CRITERIA

Disciplined with research focus
- believe this will be most effective over the long term.

Experienced
- want a portfolio manager who has lived through more than one business and market cycle.

Seniority
- want a portfolio manager who has made a long-term committment to the firm and will be around in the future;
- the firm must be able to demonstrate stability of key personnel.

Bottom-line orientation
- net returns, after all fees and charges are what is important.

As a first screen, the chairman developed a questionnaire to get information on a firm's history, investment philosophy and performance track record. With this information, he felt he could narrow the list of potential managers to a reasonable size for personal interviews.

CASE STUDY FOUR

John White, an entrepeneur in his early fifties, recently sold sixty percent of his business to a large multi-national company. He has retained forty percent of the ownership and has signed a five year management contract. John has little experience with investing in the stock and bond markets since he always put whatever money he made back into the business. As a result, both John and his wife Susan find themselves overwhelmed by the prospect of managing this capital themselves and have decided to retain the services of an investment counselor. Since John is still working full-time, Susan will handle most aspects of the manager search.

John and Susan have some biases about the type of firm they want to hire. First, and most importantly, the firm must realize that Susan has an equal say in the decision-making, and will not only handle the manager search but will be the key contact person in the relationship. Also, they want to feel as important or more important to the firm and to the account manager as any of the other clients. They would prefer that both the firm and the account manager have extensive experience with taxable clients and that these clients represent a significant part of the firm's overall business. Susan and John are both well educated and widely travelled and want international diversification in their portfolio.

Although there won't be any income requirements from the portfolio immediately, John and Susan feel they must take a reasonably conservative approach to the management of these assets. This is the capital they will have to depend on for their retirement income since they will not have company pensions. They also realize that inflation and taxes will take a significant chunk of any investment returns earned. They would like to achieve at least a real return of 2% to 4% percent after taxes and after inflation.

PRELIMINARY INVESTMENT POLICY STATEMENT

OBJECTIVES
- Real after-tax, after-inflation return of 2% to 4%;
- Conservative, long term approach;
- No income requirements for three to five years.

CONSTRAINTS
- No significant constraints although John and Susan feel they should be reasonably ethical and environmentally responsible in their investments.

TIME HORIZON
- These assets will need to be managed for the remainder of their lives, at least twenty-five years and probably longer.

SIZE
- The proceeds from the sale of the sixty percent interest in the company is approximately three million dollars after-tax.

In sorting out their priorities in the selection of a manager and the firm, it quickly became apparent that the personal issues would take priority. Susan is concerned that any individual and firm treat her as they would treat any male client and that she has the opportunity to learn more about the long term issues that affect the investment portfolio. She would like to feel comfortable asking questions and expects to get serious answers.

CHARACTERISTICS/CRITERIA

Service
- this is the most important criteria
- personalized attention and a high degree of empathy with the account manager

Established track record
- demonstrated ability to do a good job over the long term;
- good track record in managing their own business.

Conservative
- important to keep what they have so don't want undue risks taken.

Commitment to Private Wealth
- firm should have a significant part of their business in
  this area and devote substantial resources to this business area.

Due to the strong focus on the service relationship John
and Susan feel they will likely be happiest with a small
to medium sized firm. They don't believe in the "big is
beautiful" school of thought and would prefer to be one
of a small select number of clients. Since there is such
a wide selection of firms to choose from they will probably eliminate those that receive revenue from trading
commissions or corporate finance work.

CASE STUDY FIVE

Mrs. Smith is what many people have always considered
the classic investment management client. She is sixty-
nine years old and was widowed six months ago. Mrs.
Smith was left very well-off by her husband but the past
six months have been a strain. As her husband's executrix
she has had to deal with many financial issues that are
new to her. Although she has always managed the family's cash flow, her husband took care of the investments.

Mrs. Smith has received a great deal of help from her lawyer, Mr. Jones, in dealing with her husband's estate and
gathering all the information about their joint affairs. She
was quite surprised to find that, in addition to her home,

her net worth is over one million dollars. She and her husband owned a duplex which they rented, plus GIC's, a few high quality stocks, mutual funds and Canada Savings Bonds.

After seriously considering both her capabilities and interests, Mrs. Smith has decided to sell the duplex immediately. She prefers to have her time available for golf, tennis, skiing and travelling rather than worrying about an income property.

Mrs. Smith has a close relationship with her children and grandchildren, who will inherit the estate, but they are not financially dependent on her. She considers her income requirements to be moderate and expects to need after-tax income of $2,000 per month to supplement her pension income.

Since Mr. Smith handled all their investments, she is at a loss as to what she should do. The broker her husband dealt with has advised her that it is unwise to simply buy and hold stocks, since even blue chip stocks need monitoring. She knows her husband spent a lot of time following the stock market and she isn't sure how much time she wants to devote to it. In addition she is worried about her capabilities and lack of experience in this area.

After worrying about it for a few months, she has decided the safest action is to sell the stocks and mutual funds and invest the money in GIC's. That way she can be sure she won't lose anything.

Before instructing the broker to sell her holdings, she decides to discuss her decision with her lawyer, Mr. Jones.

While her lawyer agrees that this course of action will eliminate the day-to-day management of her investments and protect the capital, he raises a concern about the lack of growth in the capital to offset any erosion caused by inflation.

Mr. Jones suggests that a more appropriate solution would be to hire an investment manager who will take care of the day-to-day management of a fully diversified investment portfolio. Since he has some knowledge of firms that provide this service he can assist in selecting the manager and monitoring the service on an ongoing basis.

Together, Mrs. Smith and Mr. Jones developed a preliminary Investment Policy Statement.

PRELIMINARY INVESTMENT POLICY STATEMENT

OBJECTIVES
- Preservation of the real value of the capital;
- After-tax income of $24,000 per year with the potential for this to increase;
- Modest potential for real growth in the capital to benefit her heirs;
- Conservative stewardship of the estate her husband built.

CONSTRAINTS
- No ethical, moral or legal constraints;
- Should maintain sufficient cash cushion to accommodate spur of the moment trips.

TIME HORIZON
- The time horizon is the remainder of Mrs. Smith's life, probably between ten and twenty-five years.

After considering Mrs. Smith's objectives, Mr. Jones developed the following criteria to narrow the number of potential firms.

CHARACTERISTICS/CRITERIA

Experienced
- believe that only someone with at least fifteen years experience has seen both the ups and downs.

References
- would feel most comfortable making a referral to a firm that can offer references from other clients with similar objectives.

Team approach
- uncomfortable with single individual approach.

Service
- since this is new to Mrs. Smith a lot of service may be required initially.

Fee only
- believe it is best to eliminate any potential conflicts of interest.

Empathy
- for Mrs. Smith to be happy she will need to feel that the manager has empathy for her situation;
- she likes to think of her professional advisors as friends.

Reporting
- the manager must be prepared to provide reports to
  Mr. Jones to assist in his on-going monitoring of the
  relationship.

Mr. Jones had decided to conduct preliminary interviews
with eight firms, consisting of two small firms, two mid-
size firms and four large firms, including both independent firms and financial institutions. From these eight he
will chose three or four based on their experience, investment track record, management history and stability
and who the account manager will be. From this list Mrs.
Smith can interview and select whichever firm she feels
most comfortable with.

Chapter Eleven

Conclusion

As you can see through the case studies in the preceding chapter, hiring the "best" money manager is not difficult. By focusing on your objectives, it can be a manageable task. You may want to have your lawyer, accountant or other professional advisor or a trusted friend help with the information gathering. Since you will be the one who has to live with the decision, it is important that you participate fully in the process.

It is not surprising that, in the past, many people have left the responsibility for choosing a manager to others, or made decisions based on inadequate or incomplete information. The investment industry has not always made an effort to educate clients or to be user-friendly.

Clients of investment services are better educated than ever before, and expect more from their investment manager. Clients expect both excellent service and excellent investment performance. This book will help clients be knowledgeable consumers of discretionary investment management services. By knowing what information to look for and why that information is important, you will have increased the probability of making a good decision the first time and having a successful relationship with your manager. By focusing on your investment objectives and hiring the investment manager best able to meet those objectives, you will ensure your financial well-being.

GLOSSARY

Bond — A certificate issued by a government or public company promising to repay money borrowed at a specified rate of interest for a defined period of time. Normally, assets are pledged as collateral for a bond issue except in the case of government bond issues.

Book value — The original purchase price of a security including any commissions paid on the purchase.

Capital — Accumulated wealth or money that is invested in the ownership of companies or real property, or lent at interest.

Capital gains or losses — Profits or losses earned by selling an investment at a price higher or lower than the purchase price.

Commercial Paper — Short term negotiable debt securities issued by non-financial corporations with terms of up to one year.

Common equities — Shares representing the ownership interest of common shareholders in a company.

Convertible debentures — A debenture that can be converted into another form of security, usually the common stock, of the issuing company at a specified price or ratio. For example, one par value $1000 bond convertible into fifty shares of common stock.

Debentures — A certificate of indebtedness of a government or company backed only by the general credit of the issuer and unsecured by specific assets.

Dividend — An amount distributed from a company's earnings to its shareholders in proportion to the number of shares held. Over time a preferred share dividend remains at a fixed amount. The amount of a common share dividend will fluctuate with the company's earnings.

Duration — A measure that accounts for all cash flows expected from a bond. It is a weighted average term-to-maturity where the cash flows are in terms of their present value.

Fixed income securities — Securities that generate a predictable stream of interest or dividend income, such as bonds, debentures and preferred shares.

Intrinsic value — The inherent or essential value of a security which can differ from the current market value.

Liquidity — The ability of the market in a particular security to absorb a reasonable amount of buying or selling at reasonable price changes.

Market value — The current market price of a security.

Maturity — The date on which a bond or debenture comes due and is to be paid off.

Money Market — That part of the capital market in which short term financial obligations are bought and sold.

Mutual fund — A fund that uses its capital to invest in other securities. The fund can be structured as a company or a trust and the public can purchase and redeem units or shares directly.

Portfolio — Holdings of securities by a client. A portfolio will contain securities of different types from a number of issuers.

Preferred equities — Shares representing the ownership interests of preferred shareholders in a company and entitling the owners to a fixed dividend payment.

Securities — certificates representing ownership of stocks, bonds or debentures.

Time-weighted Rate of Return — A method of calculating the total return of investments which neutralizes the impact of differing cash flows. It allows for direct comparisons of returns from portfolios with different cash flows and is the only acceptable method of calculating returns for performance reporting.

APPENDIX ONE

ASSOCIATION FOR INVESTMENT MANAGEMENT AND RESEARCH
5 Boar's Head Lane
P.O. Box 3668
Charlottesville, Virginia   Phone: (804) 977-6600
22903 U.S.A.   Fax: (804) 977-1103

CANADIAN SOCIETIES AND CHAPTERS

Calgary Society of Financial Analysts

Edmonton Society of Financial Analysts

Montreal Society of Financial Analysts

Toronto Society of Financial Analysts
    Atlantic Chapter of the Toronto Society of Financial
    Analysts
    The Ottawa Chapter of the Toronto Society of
    Financial Analysts
        390 Bay Street, Suite 2000
        Toronto, Ontario M5H 2Y2
        Phone: (416) 366-5755   Fax: (416) 860-0580
        Executive Administrator: Francis Dvorchik

Vancouver Society of Financial Analysts

Winnipeg Society of Financial Analysts
    Saskatchewan Chapter of the Winnipeg Society of
    Financial Analysts

ASSOCIATION FOR INVESTMENT MANAGEMENT AND RESEARCH

CODE OF ETHICS AND STANDARDS OF PROFESSIONAL CONDUCT

Effective January 1, 1990
As amended May 2, 1992

CODE OF ETHICS

A financial analyst should conduct himself* with integrity and dignity and act in an ethical manner in his dealings with the public, clients, customers, employers, employees and fellow analysts.

A financial analyst should conduct himself and should encourage others to practice financial analysis in a professional and ethical manner that will reflect credit on himself and his profession.

A financial analyst should act with competence and should strive to maintain and improve his competence and that of others in the profession.

A financial analyst should use proper care and exercise independent professional judgment.

---

*Masculine pronouns, used throughout the Code and Standards to simplify sentence structure, shall apply to all persons, regardless of sex.

THE STANDARDS OF PROFESSIONAL CONDUCT

I. **Obligation to Inform Employer of Code and Standards**
    The financial analyst shall inform his employer, through his direct supervisor, that the analyst is obligated to comply with the Code of Ethics and Standards of Professional Conduct, and is subject to disciplinary sanctions for violations thereof. He shall deliver a copy of the Code and Standards to his employer if the employer does not have a copy.

II. **Compliance with Governing Laws and Regulations and the Code and Standards**

    A. **Required Knowledge and Compliance**
       The financial analyst shall maintain knowledge of and shall comply with all applicable laws, rules, and regulations of any government, government agency, and regulatory organization governing his professional, financial, or business activities, as well as with these Standards of Professional Conduct and the accomanying Code of Ethics.

    B. **Prohibition Against Assisting Legal and Ethical Violations**
       The financial analyst shall not knowingly participate in, or assist, any acts in violation of any applicable law, rule, or regulation of any government, governmental agency, or regulatory organization governing his professional, financial or business activities, nor any act which would violate any provision of these Standards of Professional Conduct or the accompanying Code of Ethics.

    C. **Prohibition Against Use of Material Nonpublic Information**
       The financial analyst shall comply with all laws and regulations relating to the use and communication of material nonpublic information. The financial analyst's duty is generally defined as to not trade while in possession of, nor communicate, material nonpublic information in breach of a duty, or if the information is misappropriated.

       Duties under the Standard include the following: (1) If the analyst acquires such information as a result of a special or confidential relationship with the issuer or others, he shall not communicate the information (other than within the relationship), or take investment action on the basis of such information, if it violates that relationship. (2) If the analyst is not in a special or confidential relationship with the issuer or others, he shall not communicate or act on material nonpublic information if he knows, or should have known, that such information (a) was disclosed to him, or would result in a breach of a duty, or (b) was misappropriated.

If such a breach of duty exists, the analyst shall make reasonable efforts to achieve public dissemination of such information.

D. Responsibilities of Supervisors

A financial analyst with supervisory responsibility shall exercise reasonable supervision over those subordinate employees subject to his control, to prevent any violation by such persons of applicable statues, regulation, or provisions of the Code of Ethics or Standards of Professional Conduct. In so doing the analyst is entitled to rely upon reasonable procedures established by his employer.

III. Research Reports, Investment Recommendations and Action

A. Reasonable Basis and Representations

1. The financial analyst shall exercise diligence and thoroughness in making an investment recommendation to others or in taking an investment action for others.

2. The financial analyst shall have a reasonable and adequate basis for such recommendations and actions, supported by appropriate research and investigation.

3. The financial analyst shall make reasonable and diligent efforts to avoid any material misrepresentation in any research report or investment recommendation.

4. The financial analyst shall maintain appropriate records to support the reasonableness of such recommendations and actions.

B. Research Reports

1. The financial analyst shall use reasonable judgement as to the inclusion of relevant factors in research reports.

2. The financial analyst shall distinguish between facts and opinions in research reports.

3. The financial analyst shall indicate the basic characteristics of the investment involved when preparing for general public distribution a research report that is not directly related to a specific portfolio or client.

C. Portfolio Investment Recommendations and Actions

1. The financial analyst shall, when making an investment recommendation or taking an investment action for a specific portfolio or client, consider its appropriateness and suitability for such portfolio or client. In considering such matters, the financial analyst shall take into account (a) the needs and circumstances of the client, (b) the basic characteristics of the investment involved, and (c) the basic characteristics of the total portfolio. The financial analyst shall use reasonable judgement to determine the applicable relevant factors.

2. The financial analyst shall distinguish between facts and opinions in the presentation of investment recommendations.

3. The financial analyst shall disclose to clients and prospective clients the basic format and general principles of the investment processes by which securities are selected and portfolios are constructed and shall promptly disclose to clients any changes that might significantly affect those processes.

D. Prohibition Against Plagiarism

The financial analyst shall not, when presenting material to his employer, associates, customers, clients, or the general public, copy or use in substantially the same form material prepared by other persons without acknowledging its use and identifying the name of the author or publisher of such material. The analyst may, however, use without acknowledgement factual information published by recognized financial and statistical reporting services or similar services.

E. Prohibition Against Misrepresentation of Services

The financial analyst shall not make any statements, orally or in writing, which misrepresents (1) the services that the analyst or his firm is capable of performing for the client, (2) the qualifications of such analyst or his firm, or (3) the expected performance of any investment.

The financial analyst shall not make, orally or in writing, explicitly or implicitly, any assurances about or guarantees of any investment or its return except commnication of accurate information as to the terms of the investment instrument and the issuer's obligations under the instrument.

F. Performance Presentation Standards

1. The financial analyst shall not make any statements, oral or written, which misrepresent the investment performance that the analyst

or his firm has accomplished or can reasonably be expected to achieve.

2. If an analyst communicates directly or indirectly individual or firm performance information to a client or prospective client, or in a manner intended to be received by a client or prospective client ("Performance Information"), the analyst shall make every reasonable effort to assure that such performance information is a fair, accurate and complete presentation of such performance.

3. The financial analyst shall inform his employer about the existence and content of the Association for Investment Mangement and Research's Performance Presenation Standards, and this Standard III F, and shall encourage his employer to adopt and use the Performance Presentation Standards.

4. If Performance Information complies with the Performance Presentation Standards, the analyst shall be presumed to be in compliance with III F 2 above.

5. An analyst presenting Performance Information may use the following on the Performance Information presenation, but only if the analyst has made very reasonable effort to assure that such presentation is in compliance with the Performance Presentation Standards in all material resepcts:

This Report has been prepared and presented in compliance with the Performance Presentation Standards of the Association for Investment Management and Research.

This Standard shall take effect January 1, 1993.

G. Fair Dealing with Customers and Clients

The financial analyst shall act in a manner consistent with his obligation to deal fairly with all customers and clients when (1) disseminating investment recommendations, (2) disseminating material changes in prior investment advice, and (3) taking investment action.

IV. Priority of Transactions

The financial analyst shall condust himself in such a manner that transactions for his customers, clients, and employer have priority over transactions in securities or other investments of which he is the beneficial owner, and so that transactions in securities or other investments in which he has such beneficial ownership do not operate adversely to their interest. If an analyst decides to make a recommendation about the purchase or sale of a security or other investment, he shall give his customers, clients, and employer adequate opportunity to act on this recommendation before acting on his own behalf.

For purposes of these Standards of Professional Conduct, a financial analyst is a "beneficial owner" if he directly or indirectly, through any contract, arrangement, understanding, relationship or otherwise, has or shares a direct or indirect pecuniary interest in the securities or the investment.

V.   Disclosure of Conflicts

The financial analyst, when making investment recommendations, or taking investment actions, shall disclose to his customers and clients any material conflict of interest relating to him and any material beneficial ownership of the securities or other investments involved that could reasonably be expected to impair his ability to render unbiased and objective advice.

The financial analyst shall disclose to his employer all matters that could reasonably be expected to interfere with his duty to the employer, or with his ability to render unbiased and objective advice.

The financial analyst shall also comply with all requirements as to disclosure of conflicts of interest imposed by law and by rules and regulations of organizations governing his activities and shall comply with any prohibitions on his activities if a conflict of interest exists.

VI.   Compensation

A. Disclosure of Additional Compensation Arrangements

The financial analyst shall inform his customers, clients, and employer of compensation or other benefit arrangements in connection with his services to them which are in addition to compensation from them for such services.

B. Disclosure of Referral Fees

The financial analyst shall make appropriate disclosures to a prospective client or customer of any consideration paid or other benefit delivered to others for recommending his services to that prospective client or customer.

C. Duty to Employer

The financial analyst shall not undertake independent practice which could result in compensation or other benefit in competition with his employer unless he has received written consent from both his employer and the person for whom he undertakes independent employment.

VII. Relationships with Others

A. Preservation of Confidentiality

A financial analyst shall preserve the confidentiality of information communicated by the client concerning matters within the scope of the confidential relationship, unless the financial analyst receives information concerning illegal activities on the part of the client.

B. Maintenance of Independence and Objectivity

The financial analyst, in relationships and contacts with an issuer of securities, whether individually or as a member of a group, shall use particular care in determining applicable fiduciary duty and shall comply with such duty as to those persons and interests to whom it is owed.

VIII. Use of Professional Designation

The qualified analyst may use, as applicable, the professional designation "Member of the Association for Investment Management and Research", "Member of the Financial Analysts Federation", and "Member of the Institute of Chartered Financial Analysts", and is encouraged to do so, but only in a dignified and judicious manner. The use of the designations may be accompanied by an accurate explanation (1) of the requirements that have been met to obtain the designation, and (2) of the Association for Investment Management and Research, the Financial Analysts Federation, and the Institute of Chartered Financial Analysts, as applicable.

The Chartered Financial Analysts may use the professional designation "Chartered Financial Analyst", or the abbreviation "CFA", and is encouraged to do so, but only in a dignified and judicious manner. The use of the designation may be accompanied by an accurate explanation (1) of the requirements that have been met to obtain the designation, and (2) of the Association for Investment Management and Research, and the Institute of Chartered Financial Analysts.

IX. Professional Misconduct

The financial analyst shall not (1) commit a criminal act that upon conviction materially reflects on his honesty, trustworthiness or fitness as a financial analyst in other respects, or (2) engage in conduct involving dishonesty, fraud, deceit or misrepresentation.

Amended - May 2, 1992, Standard III C,E,G, IV and VI C revised
Amended - May 2, 1992, Standard III F added

THE CANADIAN SECURITIES INSTITUTE

Suite 1550, P.O. Box 113
121 King Street West
Toronto, Ontario   Phone: (416) 364-9130
M5H 3T9   Fax: (416) 359-0486

National Bank Tower, 27th Floor
600, de la Gauchetiere W.
Montreal, Quebec   Phone: (514) 878-3591
H3B 4L8   Fax: (514) 878-2607

Suite 2330, 3 Calgary Place
355, 4th Ave. S.W.
Calgary, Alberta   Phone: (403) 262-1791
T2P 0J1   Fax: (403) 265-4603

Box 49151, Four Bentall Centre
944-1055 Dunsmuir Street
Vancouver, British Columbia   Phone: (604) 683-1338
V7X 1J1   Fax: (604) 683-6050

The Canadian Securities Institute awards the Fellow of the Canadian Securities Institute (FCSI) designation to securities industry personnel who completed the Canadian Investment Finance (CIF) Parts I and II study program prior to 1991 or complete Canadian Investment Management (CIM) Parts I and II.

Canadian Investment Management is a two year, two part study program designed to teach financial planning (CIM Part I) and investment management (CIM Part II).

REQUIREMENTS FOR THE FCSI DESIGNATION

Employment Requirement – Candidates must be employed by a Member firm of the Investment Dealers Association or The Montreal Exchange, The Toronto, The Alberta, or the Vancouver Stock Exchanges, or by one of these institutions: The Canadian Depository for Securities Limited; Trans Canada Options Inc.; or by the Institute itself at the time they apply for and receive the designation.

Education Requirement – Completion of CIM Part II or CIF Part II, and any of the Registered Representative Manual Exam, the New Partners and Directors Qualifying Exam or the Branch Manager's Exam.

APPENDIX TWO

Firms that provide descretionary investment management services can be identified through the following sources:

Canadian Chartered Banks

Foreign Banks licenced to operate in Canada

Trust Companies

Life Insurance Companies

Benefits Canada Magazine
Annual November issue
Maclean Hunter Limited
777 Bay Street, Toronto, Ontario M5W 1A7
Phone: (416) 596-5000
Single issue price: $13.00 plus G.S.T.

Canada's Money Managers
FACTS Publishing
70 York Street, Suite 950, Toronto, Ontario M5J 1S9
Phone: (416) 364-1418
Fax: (416) 947-7213
Directory price: $950.00 plus G.S.T.

INVESTMENT COUNSEL ASSOCIATION OF ONTARIO

Mr. Keith A. Douglas
Executive Director
Investment Counsel Association of Ontario
59 Shaw Street, Toronto, Ontario M6J 2W3
Phone: (416) 367-5177
Fax: (416) 367-8958

Membership list available

MEMBERSHIP ELIGIBILITY CRITERIA

The association's primary purpose is to encourage integrity, public responsibility and competence in the profession of investment counsel. Qualification for membership is prescribed below.

1. A member firm shall be a Corporation, partnership or sole proprietorship registered by the Ontario Securities Commission as investment counsel/portfolio manager under the adviser category and whose registration continues in good standing.

2. No member firm may be owned by, or affiliated either directly or indirectly with, any stockbroker, investment dealer or securities underwriter.

3. Not more than 30% of a member firm's gross revenue may be derived from other than the practice of investment counsel.

4. Not more than 25% of a member firm's gross revenue may be derived from a single client or associated clients.

5. Member firms must abide by the Function and Principles of the Profession of Investment Counsel as adopted by the Investment Counsel Association of Ontario in 1967, as they may be amended from time to time.

INVESTMENT COUNSEL ASSOCIATION OF QUEBEC

Mr. Jean-Luc Landry, B.A. (Econ.)
President
Investment Counsel Association of Quebec
c/o Bolton Tremblay Inc.
1100, University Street, Suite 800
Montreal, Quebec H3B 4K5
Phone: (514) 875-7150
Fax: (514) 878-3564

Membership list available

PURPOSE

The purposes of the Corporation are:

To regroup in an association investment counsel in order to foster integrity, public responsibility and competence in the practice of investment counsel.

To consult and co-operate with federal and provincial governments and agencies and all other intersted persons or groups for the development, formulation and enactment of legislation and regulations regulating investment counselling.

MEMBERSHIP

Qualifications. — Membership in the corporation shall be open to any investment counselling firm (whether a corporation, partnership or sole proprietorship) which is licensed as an investment advisor by the Quebec Securities Commission and which meets such requirements of experience, financial standing and integrity as the members of the Corporation may from time to time prescribe.

Admission. — Any qualified firm shall be admitted to membership upon submitting evidence satisfactory to the Board of Directors that it meets the prescribed minimum requirements as set out in the Code of the business of Investment Counsel as adopted by the Corporation and, in particular, that it is not affiliated to a stockbroker, underwriter or bank.

APPENDIX THREE

For those who wish to pursue additional information on investment policy and investment philosophies a number of excellent books are available which are highly readable.

CLASSICS
An Investor's Anthology
Edited by Charles D. Ellis with James R. Vertin
Published by: AIMR and BUSINESS ONE IRWIN

CLASSICS II
Another Investor's Anthology
Edited by Charles D. Ellis with James R. Vertin
Published by: AIMR and BUSINESS ONE IRWIN

INVESTMENT POLICY
How to Win the Loser's Game
Charles D. Ellis
Published by: Dow Jones-Irwin

These books can be ordered from the Association for Investment Management and Research.

THE NEW MONEY MASTERS
John Train
Harper & Row Publishers

INVESTING WITH THE BEST
Claude Rosenberg
Published by: John Wiley

PROFESSIONAL PORTFOLIO MANAGEMENT: IS
"STYLE" SUBSTANCE?
James A. Knowles and William R. Waters
Published in: Canadian Investment Review, Fall 1989
Available from:
Portfolio Analytics Limited
194 Merton Street, Suite 401
Toronto, Ontario M4S 1A1
(416) 489-7074

NOTES

INVESTMENT POLICIES

OBJECTIVES

_____

_____

_____

_____

_____

_____

_____

_____

_____

_____

_____

_____

_____

_____

_____

_____

_____

_____

_____

CONSTRAINTS

_____

_____

_____

_____

_____

_____

_____

_____

_____

TIME HORIZON

_____

_____

_____

TAX TREATMENT

_____

_____

_____

SIZE

_____

_____

_____

CHARACTERISTICS/CRITERIA

_____

_____

_____

_____

_____

_____

_____

_____

_____

_____

_____

_____

_____

_____

_____

_____

_____

_____

_____

_____

CHARACTERISTICS/CRITERIA

_____

_____

_____

_____

_____

_____

_____

_____

_____

_____

_____

_____

_____

_____

_____

_____

_____

_____

_____

_____

THE INSIDER'S GUIDE TO
SELECTING THE "BEST" MONEY MANAGER

Could someone you know benefit from reading *The Insider's Guide to Selecting the Best Money Manager.* It is an excellent tool for anyone involved in the hiring of an investment manager either as a client or as an advisor.

Please send _____ copies of *The Insider's Guide To Selecting The Best Money Manager* at $17.95 plus G.S.T. for a total of $19.21 each, including shipping and handling. Enclosed is a cheque payable to Rodgers Investment Consulting in the amount of $ _____ .

Full Name: _____

Company: _____

Address: _____

_____

City _____ Prov. _____

Postal Code _____

Telephone: _____

Discounts are available on orders of twenty-five or more books.

Please contact us at:
RODGERS INVESTMENT CONSULTING
12 St. Clair Avenue, East,
P.O. Box 69042
Toronto, Ontario M4T 3A1
Phone: (416) 967-4816

Please allow four to six weeks for delivery.